Finding
GOD IN A
BAG *of*
GROCERIES

★

SHARING FOOD, DISCOVERING GRACE

Finding
GOD IN A
BAG *of*
GROCERIES

★

LAURA LAPINS WILLIS

Abingdon Press
NASHVILLE

FINDING GOD IN A BAG OF GROCERIES
SHARING FOOD, DISCOVERING GRACE

Copyright © 2013 by Laura Lapins Willis

Library of Congress Cataloging-in-Publication Data has been requested.

ISBN 978-1-4267-5324-4

While all the stories in this book are true, some names and details have been changed to protect the privacy of the individuals.

13 14 15 16 17 18 19 20 21 22—10 9 8 7 6 5 4 3 2 1

MANUFACTURED IN THE UNITED STATES OF AMERICA

PRAISE FOR

Finding God in a Bag of Groceries

"If you have wondered about how you know what a good next step is, about how you find a place in God's church; if you have wondered about the connection between being fed at the altar and feeding other hungry people; if you have wondered about the ways self-knowledge intertwines with knowledge of God—if you have wondered any of those things, read this book."
—Lauren F. Winner, author of *Girl Meets God*

"In *Finding God in a Bag of Groceries*, Laura carries us on a journey through the poverty found in Southern Appalachia to the hallowed ground of the sacred. She teaches us along the way through her stories to reflect on our own poverty and to use it to find our way to God's rich love. She is authentic and dogged in her determination to channel that love to all she serves."
—Becca Stevens, founder of Magdalene and Thistle Farms, author of *Snake Oil*

"I thoroughly enjoyed *Finding God in a Bag of Groceries*. I felt as if I knew all the people, indeed as if I were right there—maybe helping bag the groceries. Willis's book is vivid and compels the reader to travel with her."
—Margaret Guenther, Episcopal priest and author of *Holy Listening* and *The Practice of Prayer*

For John

CONTENTS

CONTENTS

Chapter
ONE

STEPPING

Out-of-

BOUNDS

Be who God meant you to be
and you will set
the whole world on fire.

—SAINT CATHERINE OF SIENA

I BROKE THE RULES TODAY.

I didn't lie, cheat, or steal. But according to my church, I broke the rules.

I baptized someone.

In the tradition of the church I belong to—the Episcopal Church—rituals and protocols give our denomination its structure (many of which are found in our guidebook, *The Book of Common Prayer*). Only ordained priests are authorized to baptize people, unless in cases of emergency, such as someone dying.

But, Rebecca asked me to baptize her as we stood at the altar in the church, next to the baptismal font full of water.

She begged me to baptize her. Her mother was there, supporting Rebecca's transformation, weeping.

I couldn't say no, no matter what the rules said.

I had to baptize Rebecca.

I wanted to do it.

Rebecca had been a client for only a few months at the Community Action Committee (CAC), the outreach ministry I directed in Sewanee, Tennessee. Like many of my clients, she was low-functioning and had serious health problems. When I first met her, she was pregnant with her second child. She was in her mid-twenties but looked like a teenager—barely five feet tall with a round face, clear ivory skin, and long brown hair.

Rebecca's baby—Miriam was her name—was born prematurely the following January, with grave health problems. She spent many weeks in the hospital before Rebecca and her husband, Jason, were finally able to take her home in late February.

In early March, Miriam died. She died in her father's arms, while they sat in a rocking chair near the wood-burning stove, trying to keep warm in their small, dilapidated house. Miriam had a seizure and stopped breathing and died. Rather than call 911 and wait for an ambulance (they live in a very remote area in a deep cove with limited access), Rebecca and Jason put Miriam in the car and drove her twenty-five minutes to the nearest hospital, a facility that mostly provides triage for our rural community. She didn't breathe during the entire trip.

Miriam was airlifted to Chattanooga, where doctors and nurses brought her back to life. She spent almost fifty days in the ICU. Jason and Rebecca lived at the Ronald McDonald House adjacent to the hospital, sixty miles from home, coming back to Sewanee occasionally to see their older daughter and to get a few things.

On one of their trips home, Rebecca came to see me. She wept as she told me about how many machines Miriam was connected to, how she longed to hold her baby girl, how she hated being away from home, how she worried about Miriam's life (and death), how she appreciated Jason through this crisis, and how she wished her own mother could come help her. All I could do was listen quietly, offer empathetic murmurs of hope, offer her tissues as she cried, and give her a sack of food for her older child. I encouraged Rebecca to find the hospital chaplain when she returned to Chattanooga. She needed to talk to someone with a lot more training than I to help her with the tragedy unfolding in her family's life.

Miraculously, Miriam came home in June, connected to tubes and monitors and all kinds of devices to help keep her alive. Rebecca proudly told me how she and Jason had been trained on the equipment and that they knew how to care for her. Home health nurses came by to help them, too.

I silently worried about Rebecca's ability to handle complex equipment and complicated instructions. I worried about her ability to cope with the needs of a severely disabled infant. The MRIs were inconclusive about brain damage, but Miriam's weight had dropped and she was being fed only through a tube. But Rebecca was delighted to be home and to have the chance to mother her new baby. We prayed together for God to give Rebecca strength to carry on.

A week later, Rebecca came to see me again. This time, she was hysterical and overwhelmed. She hadn't slept in days, and it showed. Her eyes were dull, her hair disheveled, and she was wearing a dirty T-shirt, pajama bottoms, and flip-flops. Her mother, Norma, had arrived from the Midwest and was helping, but Rebecca said she didn't know how long she could go on with this exhausting and difficult life.

"Maybe they are better off without me," she said.

"You are a precious child of God," I told her as I locked my eyes to hers. "God gave you Miriam for a reason—she needs you. Take care of yourself and get the rest you need. Your family loves and cares for you, and I do too." I sent Rebecca straight to her physician and her therapist, who put her on antidepressants and antianxiety drugs.

Just a few weeks later, Rebecca and Norma came by. Miriam was doing great and was at home with Jason. Rebecca was as bright and cheerful as I'd ever seen her. She had gotten dressed up to come into town, had put on makeup and fixed her hair, and her spirit was bright. Rebecca told me she had "found Jesus." She said that Jesus would forgive her sins if she accepted him.

This kind of talk is uncomfortable for me. It seems so based in emotion. I would much rather consider God in my head, and less in my heart. But I listened and nodded. I could hear in her voice that something had changed.

Our conversation turned to prayer. Rebecca said she didn't know how to pray and asked me if I could tell her how I learned to pray. I told her about contemplative prayer—all God asks us to do is to open up a space in our hearts for God, and God is already there. I described to her how she could begin by sitting quietly for twenty minutes, clearing her mind, and opening herself to God.

"There's a Monday night group of people who pray this way together in our church," I told her. "Maybe you'd like to come sometime." She said she would, and I told her I'd show her where they met so if I wasn't there, she wouldn't be intimidated by not knowing her way around.

The office phone was ringing and I knew it was time to wrap things up. I asked if they would like to pray together. We pulled our folding chairs close and held hands as Norma started. She offered a lovely prayer giving thanks for Rebecca and Miriam and for CAC.

"You next," Rebecca whispered after Norma finished. I did the best I could, thanking God for the life of this family. Rebecca then prayed heartfelt words of thanksgiving and asked Jesus to forgive her sins. When she finished, I closed by saying the Lord's Prayer, inviting them to join in. Norma voiced the words with me, and Rebecca started, but then stopped after the first lines. I didn't look up to see what was going on. I assumed she was overcome with emotion. We all were.

After the final "Amen," Rebecca looked up at her mother and said, "I wish I knew all of that prayer. It's so pretty. I should learn it."

Oh, sweet girl, wholly unchurched. She didn't know the words to the Lord's Prayer. Those of us who go to church, or grew up in homes where families did, take this prayer for granted. This is the first prayer we teach our toddlers, and I assumed that everyone taught it to their children, but it was foreign to Rebecca. She was ashamed, but I said that of all the prayers she could learn, this was a good one to know: it pretty much covered all the bases if you didn't know what to pray. Norma said she'd teach it to Rebecca.

I handed them each a bag of groceries from the corner of my office and offered to help them to their car. As we got to the parking lot, I asked, "Do you want to see where the contemplative prayer group meets?" We walked over and went inside the church.

Rebecca and Norma oohed and aahed over the beautiful sanctuary of our little parish church, even in the dim light of that rainy day. It is lovely, sacred space—I failed to appreciate its beauty fully since I was there almost every day. I turned on the lights, showed them where the prayer circle would be, and described how the group worked.

While I was talking, the two women were staring at the altar and the altar rail, looking a bit confused.

"What happens here?" Rebecca asked, touching the smooth, polished oak wood of the rail.

"This is where we take Communion," I said.

"I'm sorry, I don't know what that is," Rebecca said quietly.

"The crackers," her mother whispered under her breath, seeming a bit embarrassed that she had to explain this to her daughter.

So I described Communion to Rebecca, not in fancy "priest language" by calling it the Holy Eucharist, but using the stories I thought they would know. I described the Last Supper, and how Jesus promised us that He would be present to us in the breaking of the bread and the sharing of the cup.

"Each week," I said, "we gather here and do this," and I acted out the priest's role, moving around the altar rail offering invisible bread to the invisible hungry, saying the words I so deeply longed to say at Sunday services with real bread: "The body of Christ, the bread of heaven." Then I did my usual part in this rite, holding an invisible chalice, offering invisible wine to the thirsty. "The blood of Christ, the cup of salvation." I told them of the explicit connection between this sacramental act on Sundays and our ministry at CAC.

"When we pack those grocery bags you take home each time you come here, we have blessed them the same way the priest blesses the bread and wine at Communion. It is the same thing," I said, "Jesus among us and with us and in us."

I stopped talking. The altar was quiet yet it was vibrating with the energy of the Holy Spirit swirling around us as we stood in silence, contemplating the power of those words and actions, those promises of God.

"Can I come to church here and take Communion?" Rebecca asked.

"Yes, of course," I said. "Have you been baptized?" I added.

"No, but I want to be," Rebecca said expectantly. "Jason and I both want to be, and we want Miriam and Susannah to be. Can you baptize us?"

My throat closed and my heart leapt. I blinked back the tears from my eyes.

"Can you baptize us?"

All these years I had been waiting and watching for a sign that God wanted me to do something more in the church. All this time of holding steady and being faithful I yearned for a signal from God about my calling. Was this it? Would I now know what I was supposed to do? I wanted to burst into tears and declare, "Finally." With her question, Rebecca seemed to be offering me the answer I was looking for.

As I'd told Rebecca, feeding people wholesome groceries is much like offering people the bread and wine during Communion at church. But I wanted God to tell me that I should be an ordained priest, that God wanted me to baptize people. Maybe this was my burning bush, my neon sign, my phone call from above.

"Can you baptize us?"

And then the rumble of thunder from the storm outside returned me to reality.

We were standing in the cool, empty church, and the baptismal font was full of water. But there were no witnesses, no church full of believers and friends, no one else to help Rebecca in her journey if I baptized her right then. There was also no one to stop me. But where was her family? Where was her support system? Isn't that an important part of the baptismal service, when the congregation gets to have its voice? Did Rebecca even know what she was asking for? For teens and adults, baptism often comes after weeks and weeks of study and preparation. Rebecca had done none of that.

In a flash, I recalled the baptisms I'd been a part of in the past. My own two baptisms, each so different: one a sprinkling by my parents' choice, one a full immersion of my own decision. My older son Addison's baptism at the Easter Vigil, full of fragrant lilies that decorated the church. My younger son Aaron's baptism on All Saints' Day, surrounded by infants who would grow up to be his closest friends. Both boys were in starched baptismal gowns, cradled in our arms, wrapped in the sweet smell of baby. I remembered the baptisms I witnessed as a teenager doing mission work in Brazil—people gathered at the side of a cool stream, wading waist deep, in their everyday clothes, into the muddy swirling waters to feel the presence and power of God's Holy Spirit. I remembered the celebratory baptisms of my godsons. The baptisms of friends. Each event had a flavor of its own—a style depending on the time and place.

Then another array of thoughts went through my mind. First I thought, *Yes. I can baptize you because God has called me as His own and I am part of God's community. Of course, I can baptize you. Let's get started.*

That was quickly followed by: *No. I can't baptize you. I'm not a priest, not authorized by the powers of the Episcopal Church. They decide who does and who does not get to baptize or celebrate the Eucharist or anything else. I have to get someone else. You have to wait.*

Then, I had a devious thought: *Yes, I can baptize you, but let's not tell. I'm breaking the rules if I say yes, but I don't care.*

In my heart, at the purest point I can know, I wanted to do something—anything—to help this poor, suffering girl. Her baby was going to die. Her mother would leave. Her husband wasn't with her to support her in this time of crisis. Who would be with her but God? If I could help bring her closer to God through baptizing her, I would do that. By my presence, she could have a positive experience with God, or the church, that might sustain her in the future. On the flip side, if I said no she might never come back to a church.

Of course, it was ridiculous to think I was the only person who could bring her to God. Wouldn't God find her whenever God wanted, without me?

At that moment, I wasn't so sure.

So I said to her, "Rebecca, more than anything in this world, I want to be a priest so I can do just that, so I can baptize people and offer the bread at Communion. But because I'm not a priest, I'm not allowed to do that." I wanted to cry out and tell her my story of struggle and heartbreak and confusion about my calling, but this time wasn't about me, and my story wasn't a part of this day.

Norma and Rebecca looked at me, confused. They didn't understand Episcopal Church policies and hierarchy. In their tradition, if someone wants to be baptized, you take them down to the nearest creek and get on with it. As I saw their puzzled faces, I got mad at myself for the ridiculous words I had just said to this dear girl, this child of God, asking for something I seemed unwilling to give her because of a rule in an organization she'd never understand.

I took a deep breath and began my rule-breaking. I knew I was venturing into the unknown, but I didn't feel alone or as if I was doing anything other than what God was leading me to do.

"You know what," I said, "I can't baptize all your family, but . . ." I paused as I prepared to commit this act of faith,

"I can baptize you today. I'm not supposed to, but I don't think God will mind. We have a service we like to use," and I reached for two copies of the *Book of Common Prayer*. I quickly found the page where the baptism service begins, handed one red-bound book to Norma, and showed her where to follow along. Rebecca looked on with me as I explained to her that the important part of being baptized was to listen carefully and answer the questions as truthfully as she could.

Silently, I was praying, *Dear God, please do not let anyone walk through the doors of the church right now. I don't want to explain this or interrupt it. There is too much love here, and You are with us. Please keep that door closed for a few minutes. Please God, let this go on.*

Some of this prayer was selfishness on my part. I didn't want to get caught breaking the rules. Mostly I didn't want to have to interrupt this beautiful experience to explain to anyone else what was going on. The people who needed to know were right there—God and Rebecca—bound together in the Holy Spirit. Norma and I were the lucky ones who got to witness it. The rain kept coming down, making a quiet patter on the roof as we began.

I asked Norma to present Rebecca for baptism. I looked deeply into Rebecca's eyes and asked her the only question that really mattered: "Do you desire to be baptized?"

"Yes!" she said clearly, without a sound of doubt in her voice.

I moved through the rubrics of the baptismal service. I was the priest for just a few minutes.

"Do you renounce Satan . . . ? Do you renounce evil powers . . . ? Do you renounce sinful desires . . . ?"

"I do," she said emphatically each time. She wasn't reading the prayer book with us, which instructs the candidate to say, "I renounce them." She was listening to my questions and answering from her heart.

"Do you turn to Jesus Christ and accept Him as your Savior?"

"Yes!" she said enthusiastically.

"Do you put your whole trust in His grace and love?"

"Yes," she said, smiling brightly through her tears.

"Do you promise to follow and obey Him as your Lord?"

"Yes." She turned more serious at this question.

I turned to Norma and asked her, "Will you support Rebecca in her life in Christ?"

"Yes," she said. They hugged each other and clung together as they both wept.

At the full white marble font, I gave a prayer of thanksgiving over the water, stirring it with my fingertips as I offered this blessing:

We thank you, Almighty God, for the gift of water.
Over it the Holy Spirit moved in the beginning of creation. . . .
We thank you, Father, for the water of Baptism.
In it we are buried with Christ in his death.
By it we share in his resurrection.
Through it we are reborn by the Holy Spirit.[1]

I love that prayer. Saying it aloud took me back to all those precious baptisms I had witnessed. Saying those words made me recall the priests dramatically pouring the water from high above the font to make a loud, splashing noise as it fell into the basin at the baptisms of my children. Even though this font was already full, as the water moved between my fingers I knew that this was the right thing to do. I loved being the person saying those words aloud in my beloved church.

And then, the time came.

I baptized Rebecca.

"Rebecca, I baptize you in the name of the Father, and of the Son, and of the Holy Spirit. Amen."

I didn't have a pretty scallop shell or silver cup to use. I simply used my God-given hand and scooped up the holy and blessed water. I felt it run through my fingers as I poured it across Rebecca's forehead, letting it drip down her head and across her face. Tears streamed from her eyes, holy water running down her temples. Together they mixed to form a veil of love. Tears flowed down Norma's face too, as if her tears were a rebaptism she shared with her daughter.

I didn't cry. Baptizing Rebecca felt like the most natural thing in the world.

Not having any chrism for the final portion of the service, I kissed my thumb to moisten it and marked the sign of the cross on her forehead, finishing the service with its most powerful words: "Rebecca, you are sealed by the Holy Spirit in baptism and marked as Christ's own forever. Amen."

When I joined the Episcopal Church in 1991, the bishop asked me these questions as part of the confirmation service:

Will you proclaim by word and example the Good News of God in Christ?

Will you seek and serve Christ in all persons, loving your neighbor as yourself?

Will you strive for justice and peace among all people, and respect the dignity of every human being?[2]

To each of these, I answered, "I will, with God's help."

In my mind, when I baptized Rebecca that day, I was simply following through with the commitment I made when I answered those questions. With God's help, I was proclaiming the good news and I was offering Rebecca God's love—this time not through a bag of groceries, but through the redeeming waters of baptism.

Most of us come to moments like these in our lives—moments when we didn't know the answer, or maybe even the question, but knew God's grace blessed our actions; moments when God directed us in ways we did not understand but that led to a richer life—to a place where we could love and serve God best.

For me, baptizing Rebecca wasn't so much a revelation of whether I should become a priest—this is a question that follows me through many seasons—but a reminder that no matter my vocational calling, my first calling is to live out Christ living in me.

Maybe you, too, encounter times that challenge you to listen to that still, small voice that comes to us when we are open to it. Perhaps like me, you have found that these occasions, however they come, are always worth honoring. They are one of the many ways God finds us when we cannot always find God.

Chapter
TWO

LOVE

Available

HERE

My goal in life is to unite my avocation with my vocation,

as my two eyes make one in sight.

—ROBERT FROST

T HE DAY I STOOD WITH REBECCA AND NORMA
in that quiet, cool sanctuary was a crossroads for me as
I contemplated my vocation and my role in the lives of others. The path that led me to that place began years before at
another crossroads.

Long before I baptized Rebecca, I had come to a place
where each of us arrives—again and again, at times more
vibrantly than others—where we have to decide which direction to go. Will it be the path that others expect of us, one
that we've publicly pronounced but secretly no longer
embrace? Will it be a path that challenges the status quo?
Will it be a path that honors our desire for life to have a

greater purpose, something more than just an assemblage of days and weeks and years? A path that responds to the great needs of the world as well as the needs of our own heart?

Maybe some people push through this opportunity without slowing down for the chance to change directions. In my life, circumstances coincided in such a way that I had to stop and consider all the variations my life could take.

After a series of events turned my world inside out—the birth of my second son, the suicide of a close friend, quitting a demanding full-time job as a grant writer—I searched for something to do that would let me balance the things I loved: my husband, my two sons, my church and my faith, and my community in Sewanee.

I decided to stay home with my boys and await the next task that God would place in front of me. Without discrediting my previous choices in work or family, I knew I wanted to do something that left a lasting impact. I wanted to figure out my part in God's kingdom in this new season. I wanted to live with purpose. As I had for several years, I contemplated whether the priesthood was the right place for me. And I searched for signs about what to do next.

I was already familiar with the Community Action Committee. CAC was begun at Otey Parish Church in 1974 to help the needy in Sewanee, a village of about three thousand people, in south central Tennessee. Home to an excellent liberal arts college, yet in the heart of southern Appalachia, Sewanee hangs in the tension between those who have abundance and those who have had few resources for generations.

The CAC office was located in an old Sunday school classroom in the parish hall, with makeshift shelves that held nonperishable food items. When it could, CAC paid a family's electric bill or helped with medical needs, but it didn't give out much money. The year before I arrived, they gave away about $9,000 for utilities and doctor bills.

When the part-time director resigned, the rector at Otey Parish asked if I would consider applying for the job.

"I don't know anything about poor people," I said, recognizing the privileged middle-class lifestyle I had always lived. "I am not a social worker. I am not very patient with other people's problems. I don't have anything in common with poor people and I don't think they'd like me very much, either."

He assured me that the job was simple: organize volunteers to pack groceries once a month, sit in the office a few hours each week, and write checks for emergency utility bills. The job was only nine hours a week, which I could easily arrange around my family's schedule: my older son, Addison, was seven and attended the local elementary school, directly across the street from the church; Aaron was three and ready to begin preschool, conveniently located in the basement of the parish hall; my husband, John, taught college classes less than a mile up the main street in town. It seemed I should consider it.

After meeting with some of the board members and inter-
viewing with the rector again, I was offered the position, and
I accepted it. I was sure this would be the easiest job I'd ever
had. Among the less prestigious jobs on my résumé were hoe-
ing cotton one hot summer in Texas, working at the mall
while in college, and filing policies at an insurance office. I
had already been a successful fund-raiser, started an environmental group in Washington, D.C., and managed the grant
making of a private foundation. How could this be any
harder than manual labor in a hot country field or working
in the pressure cooker of our nation's capital?

Little did I know that this seemingly simple job would
force me to recognize my own poverty of spirit, help me
accept that I was imperfect and unable to solve the problems
of others, and embrace my brokenness as a way of drawing
closer to Jesus.

During my decade at CAC, the ministry expanded from
"packing a few bags of groceries" to a complex organization
with hundreds of volunteers who gave away tens of thou-
sands of pounds of food each year. The massive mobile food
pantries we hosted were life-changing for the volunteers and
fed hundreds in our region who were hungry. We put roofs
on people's homes, repaired fallen-down porches, installed
ramps for older folks, fixed broken floors, and replaced
drafty windows. We sent people to college, bought books
and backpacks for students, paid band trip and senior prom
fees for kids who couldn't have gone otherwise, bought new

telephones with secret phone numbers for women who were trying to escape their abusive husbands, and put hundreds of gallons of gas in the cars of people traveling for chemotherapy, surgery, radiation, and other medical visits.

It all started by sitting in an old office behind a borrowed desk, surrounded by cases and cans of food, and ministering to whomever came through the door. People who needed someone to share their lives with. People who needed help. People who needed God.

And God met me right there, among the sickest, neediest, poorest people in my community. Because I was the first one who needed help, who needed God. I was one of those people too.

I had wondered for years if my role in living out God's calling was in the church. As a girl, I walked to church alone each week. I felt God had something special set aside for me to do there. This feeling both bewildered me and enticed me. I wondered if I could work in the church to help others see and know Christ so I might see and know God in a more intimate way. That seemed the promise of church work.

In 1991, when I moved to Sewanee, a community with an Episcopal seminary and a college governed by the Episcopal Church, it only complicated the question for me. Sewanee is full of priests of all flavors: retired priests, professor priests, priests to the small churches in the area, priests taking retreat in our small town from their large parishes, women priests, men priests, gay priests, straight priests, people studying to be priests, college students discerning the priesthood, and ordinary people like me wondering, *Should I become a priest?*

It seems if you are "good at God," everyone thinks you should be ordained.

In one of my earliest days wrestling with the priesthood, I told a longtime friend about this struggle. Her husband, Steven, is an Episcopal priest. She seemed to understand my dilemma as we talked over tea one morning. Steven came home for lunch but we kept talking as he moved through the kitchen, within earshot but giving us space as he quietly prepared his meal.

"Kelly, I just don't know if I should be a priest," I said pleadingly. I hoped she would give me the answer. I wanted anyone to give me the answer.

"I don't know, Laura," she said. "It is a big deal to become a priest. For you. And for John." She was right: my husband wasn't sure what I should do either and how it might affect our young family.

"I can't decide, and I don't hear God giving me any answer," I said.

Steven quickly spun around from the sink, where he was draining the water from a can of tuna. The smell of the fish wafted across the room to where we were sitting. It reminded me that I was hungry. He slammed the can opener on the counter, stared right at me, and in a loud voice said, "God decides if you are going to be a priest, Laura. It is not your decision."

I laughed. I thought he was interjecting himself in our conversation for the drama of it. This would not have been out of character for Steven.

"Thanks for the advice," I said, still chuckling.

He put his things down, wiped off his hands, and came and sat with us. He was not joking. He looked me deeply in the eyes.

"I'm serious, Laura. This isn't your decision. God will make it abundantly clear to you if you are called to be a priest. You don't have a lot to say about it," he said. "You will know."

He went back to making his sandwich, then slipped it into a baggie, kissed Kelly good-bye, gave me a hug, and left. Kelly and I continued our visit, but I was turning Steven's words over and over in my head.

Is it true that I will just know whether or not to be a priest—or just know about anything else for that matter? I wondered. *Will God even choose to be involved in my decisions about my role in life?* Now, many years later, I wonder if Steven was wrong. I'm glad his decision to be a priest was obvious to him. Mine is not so easy.

I talk often to a wise friend about this question of discernment: How will I know if I am supposed to be a priest? As a devout Christian who is not an ordained priest, she has a complicated, yet realistic, view. Her advice was easier to hear than Steven's, but still challenging.

"Just listen," she said. "Be still and listen to God. Listen to what your heart tells you. There is no right or wrong answer. Live a life of love and service. That's what God asks us to do. There are many different ways to do it."

I knew this was true. I'd grown up Southern Baptist, active in a youth group that took annual mission trips around the country. I'd gone to a Christian college, where I found God not in a single church or denomination but through service. I had pursued a career in the nonprofit world, where my vocation of communicating with others was another way of answering God's call to love and serve Him.

When I arrived in Sewanee, the Episcopal Church welcomed me. I joined the church and wove its liturgies and traditions into my experiences. I discovered a renewed life in Christ. I was an adult now, and I recognized that whereas God shaped my worldview, many people didn't share this perspective. In my naiveté as a young person, I had thought everyone shared my commitment to Christ and the desire for a deeper relationship with God.

I tried describing this to another friend in one of our conversations about calling.

"I feel like I've crossed some great chasm and there's no way back," I said, after realizing that I had made a lifetime of decisions to love and serve God.

"No, you can't go back, Laura. Once you choose Christ, you can't go back. You are on a new path," she said.

All those choices I'd made so far in my life: yes, I want to walk to church by myself on Sunday mornings; yes, I want to witness about Christ to others; yes, I want to organize a campuswide revival; yes, I want to join the Episcopal Church; yes, I want to raise my children in this church; yes, I want to commit to a regular prayer practice; yes, I want to serve on the staff of our church. All these added up to a life in Christ. Each decision moved to another, and the next time I looked up, I was in the heart of the church, serving the poor, recognizing I'd walked away from a life of wealth and power. I knew I was living the right life. The next choice—to be ordained or not be ordained—seemed a less simple choice, and one that would possess me for many years.

During my decade at CAC, I struggled with my desire to celebrate the Eucharist, to baptize babies, to officiate at funerals, to be a "real" priest. Throughout this struggle, God never made it clear what I should do. Yet God endowed me with the power to love, no matter what my job title was or where I lived or what background I had. Jesus gave me the opportunity to minister to and care for others, in many ways beyond the opportunities I would have had if I'd been ordained by the church. I was already ordained by God at my baptism. I was already a part of God's priesthood of believers.

Just as Jesus called the disciples to walk away from their jobs, their families, and their safe lives, we are called into places of uncertainty. But following Jesus doesn't have to be as dramatic as abandoning one's livelihood, as the disciples giving up their fishing nets. Following Jesus always starts by doing the next thing God puts in front of us.

Learning this truth does not have to happen through a classroom or church service or formal discernment process. For me, it happened in the simplest of settings: in a pantry-turned-office, in a thirdhand trailer, in the hallway at the elementary school, and on the sidewalk at the post office. It happened through conversations with concerned fathers and angry teenagers and alcoholic women. It happened with all kinds of strangers who found me.

If you asked someone waiting at my office why they were there, they would tell you, "For a bag of groceries." But I believe most people came because of the love we offered. The food was just a way to get people to walk through the door.

After all, if I had put an ad in the newspaper that read, "Free Love Available," how would people know what to expect? In our brokenness, how do we admit that it is love we need?

So I told people, "Free Food Available," and they came for that: the peanut butter, the tuna, the applesauce, and the bread. And they kept coming back. Maybe it was the excellent tomato soup, but I think it was because of the love.

Each time a group of volunteers gathered to pack those groceries—many times a month we lined up rows of used brown paper bags, set up an assembly line of folks ranging in age from four to eighty-four, and filled the bags with food—we would pray after the work was completed. My prayer was this:

> Gracious God, just as you feed us at the altar with bread and wine, thank you for feeding our friends in need. We pray that this food fills their bellies with good things to eat and that you fill their hearts with love. Amen.

I believe that when Jesus said, "I am the bread of life," He really meant it. God intends for us to eat and be satisfied and be made whole.

I also believe that recognizing our own needy places is essential to our spiritual life.

It is these parallel journeys—of feeding the poor and exploring my own yearning for God—that frame the words of this book. Because in feeding the hungry, I saw that poverty can be an absence of economic prosperity but also a spiritual emptiness. I saw my own poverty: poverty of faith, poverty of compassion, poverty of openness. I saw that God could find me in unexpected moments and that I could find God in the most unlikely places, too. Even in a bag of groceries.

Chapter
THREE

COMING

Home

The ache for home lives in all of us,
the safe place where we can go as we are
and not be questioned.

—MAYA ANGELOU

F RANCES AND CARTER GILKERSON WERE THE
first clients I met at CAC and were all the volunteers'
favorites. They were kind, generous, grateful, and loving.
They were a good reminder of why CAC existed: to help people who tried hard and yet couldn't make ends meet. People
who loved their children and their grandchildren. People
who shared food from their table with me when I was hungry and would have taken me in if I were homeless.

The Gilkersons had both worked their whole lives. Carter
had assisted in installing furnaces in houses around the
region for decades. Both of them had worked for the Sisters
of St. Mary and their convent in Sewanee—Carter as a

handyman and Frances as a cook. For years, the trailer where their family lived sat on land owned by the Sisters. With no 401(k) or pension plan at the convent, the Sisters gave Carter the deed to the land when he retired. It was the most thoughtful, important gift they could have made.

In the early days of our friendship, I didn't fully understand why Frances would ask for extra groceries or why she or Carter came by to get bread every time we were open. Frances was always scouring the open shelves for flour or cornmeal or sugar. I could tell she really cooked. Unlike many of our younger clients, Frances made everything from scratch. Sometimes for the children she fixed the boxed macaroni and cheese dinner from our grocery bags, but she wouldn't eat it herself, she said. It wasn't until one day when we had time and no interruptions that I asked her about it.

"Frances, what do you do with all this food?" I asked in a teasing way, but I also really wondered the answer to this question.

"I cook for a lot of people," Frances said.

"She cooks all the time," Carter said.

"How many people do you cook for?" I asked

"Well, there's Scott [their son-in-law] and his four kids, and Mark [their grandson] and Kim and their two kids, and me and Carter. How many is that?" Frances said.

I was counting on my fingers as she rattled it all off: five plus four plus two. Eleven people. I was about to need a third hand.

"Frances, you cook for eleven people? How many times a week do you do this?" I asked. I was shocked. I can barely get dinner on the table for four people. Cooking for a dozen at the holidays makes me slightly crazed.

"I do it every day," she said calmly, as if it were normal to cook for eleven people daily. "During the week, the kids eat breakfast and lunch at school, but I pack lunches for Mark and Scott. Then I cook supper every night. On the weekends, I make most everything for them all."

After learning that, I would tuck things away in closed cupboards to save for Frances. I would pack extra-full bags of groceries for Carter and her to take. They always took three bags: one for them, one for Scott, and one for Mark and Kim. I knew all the groceries went straight to her house and she made meals out of those basic staples. (She always wanted extra pinto beans. Pintos and cornbread were a regular meal at their house.)

One day in the first weeks of my new job, a longtime CAC board member, Pixie, and I went to Frances and Carter's for a home visit. We took groceries out to them rather than having them come to us, because Pixie wanted me to see their home.

The Gilkersons lived in a thirdhand, red-and-white trailer held together with baling wire and duct tape. It was better than the house they had been living in before I'd met them (what you and I might call a shack), but it was still awful by middle-class standards. Newer models of mobile homes feel more spacious, and a doublewide is almost like a house. But

Frances and Carter's trailer was old, small, dark, and narrow. Probably no more than twelve feet wide, it was given to them by someone who bought a new trailer and considered this one trash. Plastic grocery bags taped to the outside covered broken windows. The siding had fallen off in several places. Abandoned cars were scattered near the trailer and chickens roamed the yard.

When Pixie and I arrived, Frances greeted us warmly. The trailer door swung to the outside and we walked right into the living room. The kitchen was part of this space, on the left side of the door. Slightly bigger than an efficiency apartment kitchen, it had a four-burner stove and oven, a regular-size refrigerator, and a bit of counter space, much of it taken up with a microwave and a coffeepot. There was a small sink and a window that looked out front where the chickens rambled. In the living room were two couches up against the walls and a big soft recliner. All the upholstery was tattered and food-stained. There was no dining table in sight. Dark brown paneling, little windows, and dim bulbs in the one overhead fixture made the space dark—like twilight on a humid night.

That trip with Pixie was my first up-close, no-escaping-it encounter with real poverty. This was the first time I saw where my dear, kind clients lived. As Pixie made small talk with Frances, I just stared, looking around the room, taking in all that was before me. It wasn't unkempt, but it wasn't clean either. It had the look of a place that had never been neat or fresh. Dense cigarette smoke hung in the air, adding to the hazy aura of the room. Frances had smoked nearly her whole life.

I sat still, making mental notes of all that was around me. A small TV with a coat-hanger antenna had a gaming system hooked up to it. No books, newspapers, or magazines. No pictures on the walls. No lamps other than the fixture on the ceiling. Dishes piled up around the sink. No dishwasher. The pantry cupboard doors were ajar. Inside were staples from CAC's shelves. Frances was wearing a worn apron over her favorite khaki skirt and floral shirt. I'd seen her in that out-fit many times before. Pixie did all the talking. I was too astonished to speak. I was afraid of what might come out of my mouth. All my civility and poise were gone.

Pixie graciously said good-bye. I tried to smile and not cry. Frances invited me to come back anytime.

I didn't ever want to go back to Frances and Carter's house. I didn't want to confront the reality of the poverty in which they lived. I liked it much better when our relationship was safely ensconced in the neatness of my office at the church, where we all could ignore the fact that they lived in a hovel that made my three-bedroom house seem like a mansion.

We could set all those differences aside and just be friends in that neutral space. If I saw their trailer too often, I was afraid of the judgments I might pass or the opinions I might develop. But I also wanted to do something about getting them out of that wretched space. I was so naive, I thought they would listen to me when I encouraged them to make a change.

"You know, there's a group in town that builds houses for people who need a place to live," I told Carter and Frances one day when they came in. "It is very low-cost and they build the house for you."

"We can't afford a new house," Carter said quickly. He cut his eyes at Frances in a gentle yet firm way that said, "Stay out of this."

"But it hardly costs you anything," I continued, not really listening to Carter. "Let me talk to Dixon, the person in charge of building new houses for folks who need them. I'll get some more details for you. It would be great, don't you think?"

I spoke in the optimistic, enthusiastic voice I used when I wanted clients to reflect my excitement back to me, when I was trying to convince them of something they were unwilling to consider.

"I can even help you fill out the application," I said, as if one small step were all that was in the way.

"It'd be a waste of time," Carter replied. "We don't need a new house. Our place is just fine."

A variation of this conversation went on, back and forth, between Carter and me for many weeks. But they were unwavering in their refusal.

Frances came in by herself to see me one morning. Carter had driven her to the church—she didn't read or write or drive—but he was sick and waited out in the car.

I thought, *Great! This is my chance to get her to agree to this new house.* I was on a mission. I was sure I knew better than Carter and Frances what was right for them, and I was determined to talk them into it.

"Frances, wouldn't you like to have a fresh, new house?" I said, pleadingly. "They would build you a big kitchen with plenty of space to cook for all those people, and it would have a dishwasher and space for a big table. It would be so wonderful."

"Laura, I know you mean well, but we don't want a new house. You have to stop this. It's making Carter mad. It isn't going to happen."

This was the first and only time Frances told me what to do. And she was right. I was treating them like children, not caring about what they wanted but trying to impose my will on them. If I thought a new house would be good for them, surely they should agree with me. I was wrong.

I apologized for being so bossy, and I stopped talking about it to them, but I didn't stop talking about it to Dixon.

"Dixon, we have to build the Gilkersons a new house. You can't believe what they live in and where Frances cooks for eleven people!" I appealed to him one afternoon in his office at the college.

Dixon reminded me that as long as the Gilkersons resisted even filling out the application form—a two-page document that asked a few simple questions about finances, family situation, and land ownership—they could not be considered for a house.

Every time I walked into my own house after one of these conversations, I was possessed by guilt and anger. Why did I get to live in a clean, warm home when my clients—my friends—had to live in terrible spaces? Why wouldn't Carter and Frances let me intervene on their behalf and help them get something better? Worst of all, I was embarrassed by the wealth of my home. If the roles were shifted, how would they feel in my house? Would they stare at the walls and judge my furniture? How would I feel if they saw where I lived?

I was ashamed of the times I had complained about my own house, my selfish desires for more stuff, and my frequent whining about wanting something new. I was disgusted by how I took all my life's abundance for granted. I prayed for forgiveness for my arrogance and for my selfishness.

Sort of.

Mostly, I prayed that God would give Carter and Frances a new house.

I left my campaign for the new house aside and worked to mend my relationship with Carter and Frances. After Frances scolded me, I realized I had stepped too deeply into their personal life. It was an important lesson. People came for financial help and for food, and if they wanted counsel about an issue, they would ask for it. I should not have dispensed advice without being asked. No one likes to be nagged about how to live his or her life, with all the implied judgment that comes along with those words. I never brought up the new-house issue again.

What I didn't know is that despite his hesitancies, Dixon did not leave the new-house issue alone. He started talking about Frances and Carter's place to other people involved in the housing effort. He drove out and looked at their trailer. He looked at the other applicants in the pool being considered for the next house. Dixon's conversations set in motion a series of interchanges I'll never exactly understand, but I know God was in their midst.

Many months after we first talked about a new house, Carter came in and sat down, wearing his favorite blue pants and striped suspenders. He was beaming, a wide grin on his big, round face. He put his hand on his hip and dipped his head a bit before he spoke. His eyes were twinkly and crinkled with his smile.

"We're going to get a new house," he said calmly, as if he were telling me they'd gotten a new chicken. I jumped up from behind my desk and bounced over to him. He stood up and we hugged.

"Oh, Carter! This is great news! I'm so excited! Oh, this is wonderful!" I could hardly believe what he was telling me. I knew they needed a house more than anyone, but how did he go from sternly telling me "We don't need a new house" to

"We're going to get a new house" in just a matter of months?

Carter then told me the whole story. (He is the best storyteller I've ever known.) He told me that Dixon told a local plumber who worked on these projects that the Gilkersons would be good candidates for a new house. The plumber told the constable that Carter and Frances were thinking of a new house but weren't sure about it. The constable told the head of the Emergency Medical Services that the Gilkersons needed persuading to get a new house. Those three men—each a longtime community member, not an outsider like me—went out and drank coffee with Carter and told him that they—not me—would build them a house, and that they—not me—would ensure that it was done right and to his satisfaction, and that they—not me—would move them into the new place with as little disruption as possible.

And so it happened. Carter and Frances never filled out an application form. They never went through the interview process with the housing group's board. They never did all the things I thought they needed to do, but on their own terms they were going to get a new house.

The house was begun in June. By early November, it was clear that with a big push of volunteer time and energy, we could have the Gilkersons in before Christmas. This became our goal.

Dixon's young assistant, Skip, was the foreman for the site. Skip and a college student virtually lived on that project.

Other college students and community members came every day. Frances took iced tea or lemonade out to every group that came.

The house was built near their trailer, so the Gilkersons could watch and listen to everything going on. Carter sat in a lawn chair making conversation with the volunteers and telling the students wonderful stories about all the houses he knew in Sewanee from installing their heating systems.

When the college students had a twenty-four-hour blitz to finish the roof, Carter pulled Skip aside and said, "Do those girls really know what they are doing up there on that roof?" Skip assured Carter that the girls really knew how to put on a roof. Carter learned about women and their roles in the modern world, while we learned about the gracious hospitality that Carter and Frances offered to everyone who came through.

The entire experience was full of grace for all of us.

One Saturday near completion there was interior painting to be done, so volunteers of all ages were invited to help. Frances wanted the walls painted white, in stark contrast to the dark paneling of the trailer. I took my two boys—Aaron, who was seven, and Addison, age eleven—with me to help. They loved being in a new house. Unlike our forty-year-old house, this one smelled of fresh paint, had new fixtures and no furniture, and seemed very spacious. It was eleven hundred square feet, but with nothing in it, it felt much bigger.

By the end of our workday, both my boys were covered in paint. I wanted to get them cleaned up before they got in our van, so I went to the trailer door and asked Frances if I could turn on their garden hose. She invited us to come inside and wash at her sink. I wasn't sure this was a good idea—one of her granddaughters was in the same grade as Addison and I wanted to protect her privacy. Frances insisted, and I did not want to be rude by refusing her invitation.

"We're going inside to wash up," I said to the boys.

"No, Mom," they both said, tugging me back. They were afraid. The trailer was dark and smoky and scary-looking to them.

"No, we are going inside," I said firmly. "Mrs. Gilkerson has opened her house to us and we're going in to wash and then we'll leave."

The afternoon sun was strong, so it took our eyes a few moments to adjust to the dimness of the interior of the trailer. Blink, blink, blink. When they focused, both boys' eyes were huge as they looked around and saw what I had seen a few years earlier: a very small space, used very hard, smelling of cigarettes. Aaron was shy and scared. He grabbed my hand with his paint-covered fingers. Frances led us to the kitchen sink and made room for us to wash.

"Here you go," she said to the boys. I was embarrassed again about our judging and our relative wealth. She was being kind and they were not cooperating. I was angry at them about their behavior. What kind of mother was I if they were acting like this?

I turned on the tap and pointed it to the left, hoping for a bit of hot water, but only cold water rushed out. Aaron was impatient and uncomfortable, propped on my knee so he could reach the water. The only soap on the counter was the orange-smelling dish soap we had given out in grocery bags just a week or two ago, so I squirted that on his little hands and started rubbing the paint off.

We rinsed, letting the water run, still hoping for something warm, when Addison moved in to wash his hands.

"It's cold," he complained loudly.

"Just wash," I said, shushing him so Frances couldn't hear him sounding ungrateful. He washed, too. With no paper towels or dish towel to dry our hands on, we just wiped them on our dirty jeans.

"Thank you, Frances, for opening your house up to us," I said as the boys quickly went back outside. "You were very kind to my boys. Thank you." She hugged me and kissed me on the cheek, and I went to the van.

"That was awful, Mom," Addison said. Aaron nodded in agreement.

"Do you understand what we were doing there?" I asked them on the way back to our house. "That is how their family has lived for a long time. Can you imagine what it must be like to live in that day after day? That's why we helped paint their new house today. I'm glad you came along today and painted. I'm glad you got to see where my friends live."

We were all quiet the rest of the way home.

★

Throughout the fall, I was concerned about what Carter and Frances would do about furnishing the new space. The furniture they had in the trailer was filthy—full of fleas, smoke, dirt, and food. I thought it would be a shame to move it into the lovely new, clean house, but I couldn't figure out how to raise enough money to buy them new furniture. I also wasn't sure I could persuade them to go with me to a city to go furniture shopping, and I knew I couldn't go pick out furniture for them without their help. We had partnered with the Sisters of St. Mary to buy their appliances: dishwasher, refrigerator, washer and dryer, and microwave. But I was still concerned.

Dixon was less worried.

"Laura, we've built them a new house. We can't do everything for them. Don't worry about it. They like their furniture and will probably want to take it with them anyway," he said.

He was right. I was being too controlling. I wanted to turn the Gilkersons's house into something out of *Southern Living* magazine, and it wasn't right. It was another occasion where I was imposing my ideas on their lives.

Then, one day in mid-November, there was a message on my phone at home: "Hey, Laura. This is Paul. We're moving to Baton Rouge and our new house is about half the size of our Sewanee house—we've got all kinds of furniture to get rid of. Some of it is practically new and I wonder if CAC could use it. We need to do it this weekend, though, so we have to act fast. Call me back."

I agreed to take the furniture sight unseen: mattresses, couches, chairs, a dinette set with six chairs, a big recliner, end tables, some lamps, two dressers, and TV and microwave stands. Even some framed posters of famous paintings. It was literally everything I thought the Gilkersons needed for their new house. Now, I had to see if they wanted someone else's furniture.

"Friends, I have something I want y'all to consider," I said to Carter and Frances the next time they were in the office. "Someone has donated a bunch of furniture, enough furniture for your entire house, and it is available to you. If you want it. But, it is entirely up to you."

"That'd be fine," Carter said, in his usual understated way.

I felt like I needed to tell them more, to sell them on this idea, even though he had just agreed to what I was proposing. "It is really nice stuff. There are two couches that match that would be perfect in the living room, and a nice dining table and chairs, and there are beds for every room. And Carter, there is a nice big recliner."

"That'd be fine," Carter said again.

"That's a mighty nice gift," Frances said. I agreed. I reminded them they would have plenty of time to take out all their personal items from the trailer before it was hauled away. They simply said, "OK."

I wondered if they felt we were taking over their lives,

telling them to leave their trailer and to get new furniture. In essence, we were condemning all they'd had before. I felt terrible. I was glad we had these things to offer, but I felt I was perpetuating a hierarchy—the wealthy telling the poor what to do and how to live—that didn't benefit the Gilkersons or me or anyone else involved in this effort. I didn't know how to change this, though. The situation was what it was: those of us at CAC were in positions of power and authority and were making decisions about their future, and Carter and Frances were going along with whatever happened. I knew they had the ability to say no and mean it and be heard, and yet they never raised their voices once the house building began.

As we neared Christmas, we began making plans for the finishing touches. The furniture was ready to move in. Some members of the community bought new sheets for all the beds, new dishes and silverware for the kitchen, and cleaning and laundry supplies for the house. Others bought towels, bath mats, and shower curtains for the bathrooms. Miniblinds were installed on all the windows.

At the dedication of the new home, a retired minister offered a blessing for the house and its residents. Many of the Sisters from the convent attended. Carter thanked everyone who had made this house possible. There were Christmas cookies and punch. Someone brought the Gilkersons a fresh Christmas tree that they put up in the corner of the living room. It looked as if they'd lived in that new house forever.

★

Much as feeding the poor reminded me of my own hunger for God, creating a home for Frances and Carter was a reminder of my own desire for safe shelter, comforting surroundings, light in the darkness. The way it came about in spite of my insensitivities and attempts to control the process reminds me there is a perfect home—and I am not there yet.

"In my Father's house are many mansions," Jesus tells us (John 14:2 KJV). Whether it holds a romanticized place in our hearts or is rooted in spiritual faith, true home is something each of us longs for. We were created for nothing less.

And we all need grace on the way to getting there.

Some people in the community, especially those who drove past Frances and Carter's home each day, questioned the wisdom of building a new house for them.

"They'll trash it just like they did that trailer," one person said, not knowing them at all.

"I bet they don't know how to take care of a house," another said, never having been inside to see that Frances was good housekeeper.

"Why did they get a house? They had a place to live," said yet another.

It is so easy to judge people, to decide what's right for them, and to be certain about the lives of others. And we are often so wrong, either with our intent or our timing or both.

To this day, the Gilkersons's new house is always tidy

when I arrive, both for planned visits and for the occasional drop-in when I'm out their way. They often sit on the porch and watch cars drive by.

I stopped by one day, late in the afternoon, and Frances was starting to cook dinner for her clan. She was making salmon patties, using the generic canned salmon she'd gotten from CAC. She was cooking the croquettes in the biggest cast-iron skillet I'd ever seen, frying them in pure lard, and the house smelled delicious. I commented that I never made salmon patties because no one in my house liked them but me and they are a lot of trouble for one person.

"Taste one," she said.

"Oh, I don't want to take one from your family," I said. "I know you have a lot to make."

"It's OK. Taste one. I want you to have it."

I realized it would be rude to refuse to share their meal.

Frances put it on a plate and handed it to me. The patty was crispy and lightly browned on the outside, and when I broke it open, it was pink and tender on the inside, steaming hot. I put a small bite on the fork and blew on it to cool it a bit. Frances and Carter watched me intently.

When I put that bit of fish into my mouth, it was Holy Eucharist. It was a feeling of the Spirit rushing throughout my body. It was communion with my friends, communion with good food, communion with God. It was the sharing of a journey, finding home.

Chapter
FOUR

MY

Calling

CARD

The mystery of poverty is that by sharing in it, making
ourselves poor in giving to others, we increase
our knowledge of and belief in love.

—DOROTHY DAY

W E EACH CARRY SYMBOLS WITH US, MARKERS OF
our vocation or our passion in life. The toolbox of a
carpenter, the diaper bag of a new parent, the cross around
my neck—we hold tight to these talismans.

Brown paper grocery sacks were the symbol of my ministry. They were always double-bagged so they could hold
canned goods, peanut butter, macaroni and cheese, cereal,
soup, snacks for kids, and shelf-stable milk—all things I
knew my friends could use in homes filled with a lot of people, not much money, and no spare time.

When I made visits, often people looked at me quizzically
and asked, "You brought groceries?"

"I always bring groceries," I'd say.

My calling card was a bag of groceries.

I went nowhere without them. I often kept a bag or two in the back of my van, just so I could stop in and see people whenever I needed to. It felt rude to show up to anyone's house empty-handed, even for a quick visit. To work at a food pantry and not bring food when I visited would have been unthinkable. Even the most reclusive of people usually welcomed me when I knocked on the door with a bag of groceries in my arms. If they weren't home, I could leave the bag on the stoop and they would know I had come by.

It was my way of showing I cared. More than that, it was a way of showing them God cared. Just as a minister wouldn't make a home visit without a Bible, and an Episcopal priest wouldn't visit the sick without a small Communion kit, I never went anywhere without a bag of groceries.

It was a cool, sunny October day in my second or third year at CAC when Tom Macfie and I agreed to make a joint pastoral visit to one of my clients who had stage IV cervical cancer. This was not something we did often—he, the rector and sole clergy at Otey, a growing church with many needs, and me, the part-time layperson charged to care for the needy in the community—but it felt like the right thing to do on that pretty day. Tom and my client, Florence, had sons who were about the same age but who had parted ways in middle school when one went to private school and the other stayed in the public school system.

On that day, Tom was in his clericals—black pants and a black shirt, with that white collar, the powerful, universal symbol of priesthood. I was dressed in what I came to think of as my uniform: jeans, a plain white cotton top, a small silver James Avery cross, and clogs. As I became more aware of the abundances of my personal life, even in the clothing I wore, I tried to bridge the gulf between me and my clients by dressing simply.

As we were getting ready to leave, Tom said, "I think I'll bring my Communion kit, in case Florence wants to receive."

"Sure," I responded distractedly, as I grabbed two bags of groceries.

We drove out of the village of Sewanee into an area of amazing natural beauty—a lovely hardwood forest, with spectacular views of the valley peeking through the trees on either side of us. Sometimes a large, expensive house was set back on the edge of the mountain, with only the driveway and the entrance visible from the road; next door might be a used mobile home set up on cinder blocks with a chain-link dog pen and trash littering the lot. Poverty abuts affluence, over and over again, down that road.

As we drew closer to her house, Tom asked if I thought Florence would want to take Communion. My unenthusiastic "sure" back at the office must have belied my true feelings about what I thought would happen on our visit. I had to be honest with him.

"No, I don't think she'll want it, Tom," I said. "She's a Christian, but in her tradition, Communion isn't central to her worship. I don't think it would mean much to her." I hated to say this because I knew how much the Eucharist meant to him and to me, but I knew it to be true, even having known Florence for only a few years.

After turning off the main road, and then turning again, we found Florence's house. It was a small, frame building with a skinny front porch. The house had once been yellow, but the paint was faded and peeling now, so it had a sickly, ashen look to it. The lawn was mowed but children's push toys were strewn about. A junked car had been abandoned in the yard, and the sidewalk only came halfway from the house to the gravel parking area. Two dogs barked to announce our arrival. Had I not visited before, I would have been scared, but I knew they were not going to bite. I opened the back of my van and I asked Tom to give me a hand with the groceries.

I felt secure walking into someone else's home bearing the gift of food. Perhaps Tom felt the same way about his antique black leather box containing miniature cruets of wine, holy water, and small pieces of consecrated bread.

With our arms loaded with nourishing things for the body and spirit, Tom and I made our way up the sidewalk, past the broken-down car, and up the three steps to the front door of the house, the dogs following us all the way.

Florence was nearing the end of her life, having fought a yearlong battle with cancer. The mother of three children and only fifty years old, she was not ready to die. She imagined herself living a much longer life. Her husband and the father of her children had died almost ten years ago, so she had raised the kids alone and wasn't prepared to leave them as orphans.

We were greeted by a hospice nurse, who had just bathed Florence. I watched Tom's eyes as he surveyed the chaotic poverty in which Florence and her family lived. An enormous television sat in the midst of the toys and debris created by a house full of distracted people. In the kitchen, there wasn't a clear place or a flat surface for us to put the groceries. There were dirty dishes in the sink and on the counters, trash spilling out of the wastebasket, open boxes of cereal, and many piles of paper and bills. It was evident that something was amiss in this house. Poverty and death together create quite a mess.

Tom and I said nothing as we moved things aside to put the groceries on the kitchen table, and then we went back to wait for Florence. Her family was large and all depended on her: Kyle, a junior in high school; Jeffrey, who worked as an electrician; and Nora, who had four children before she was twenty-eight. Nora was both working and going to school, and her children went to daycare or elementary school each day. When Tom and I arrived, the house was quiet, but it had a pulsing, frenetic energy from all those people living in what must have been fewer than eight hundred square feet. Eight people in eight hundred square feet. No wonder it felt chaotic. The littlest children slept on the floor and on the sofas because there weren't enough beds.

Florence's bright voice broke the quiet: "Father Tom, you came to see me!" Clean and refreshed, Florence rolled into the living room in a wheelchair with an enormous smile on her face. Tom coming with me was a delightful surprise for her, so I sat back, silent. This was Tom and Florence's time together: they talked intimately, sharing stories about their sons. Tom shared his hopes and dreams for Kyle, much as an uncle or dear family friend would confide in a mother. Tom's generous words made Florence laugh, the laugh of a proud momma who loves her children.

"Kyle is so smart, and people love him," Tom said. Florence wept as he offered this tender, generous compliment.

"Please take care of Kyle," she said. Their conversation continued quietly for a few more minutes, until Florence started to tire. She'd always been a woman with deep feelings, and all this emotion was wearing her out.

Tom moved away so I could take his place next to Florence. Our conversation was just a continuation of the dozens of conversations we'd had over time: "How are you? How is Nora? What do you need? How can we help? Are your bills OK? What about transportation? Are the doctors and hospice caring for you well?"

Then I said all the things to her that I'd said before, but I wanted her to know yet again: "I love you. God loves you. You have been a wonderful mother to your children and grandchildren. They will be cared for and loved by our community. Your life has been a gift to me, our friendship a treasure. I have learned so much from you. I love you."

As I spoke these words Florence was sobbing and tears were streaming down my cheeks. She was exhausted, and I knew we were near the end of our visit—and quite possibly, of our time together. It must have been near noon because Jeffrey walked into the house with two of Nora's smallest children. The energy around us changed rapidly. One child was asking for juice; another saw a cereal box peeking out of the bag we'd brought and was crying for someone to open the Apple Jacks. The children demanded that the TV be turned on. It was time to go, in so many ways.

Tom moved to the other side of Florence's wheelchair and asked if we could pray together before we left. Tom and I placed our hands on Florence's shoulders and the three of us prayed.

Tom prayed loving and beautiful words on that sad day; I must have prayed something out loud, but I don't know what I said. Florence absorbed it all—Tom's words and my words, the weight of our hands, God's love that was shining through the moment—her shoulders heaving as she continued to cry, whispering "Thank you, Jesus" and "Yes, Lord" as we prayed.

I can still recollect the intensity of the love that was flowing through us. The Holy Spirit was swirling around us, filling us with grace. Even with the television blaring and two toddlers wildly running around, God's love vibrated through the three of us like a current of beautiful power.

Our good-byes were hurried and brief. The arrival of her family meant Florence had to concern herself with caring for the others. Maybe she was also embarrassed to be so emotional in front of her son and her grandchildren. Maybe she was just tired. So I hugged the little ones good-bye and Tom and I walked back to my van.

On the drive into town, both Tom and I were silent. I was overwhelmed by the impending death of a woman I loved and admired; Tom later told me he was overwhelmed by the poverty of their situation. Both of us were moved deeply by the experience.

That was the last time I saw Florence alive. She died a few weeks later, at home, her family surrounding her. It was her youngest son, Kyle, barely seventeen years old, who spoke for the family at the funeral, handling this tragic loss with maturity and grace, carrying on that flow of intensity, power, and love.

Visiting Florence that day with Tom provoked again the questions that have followed me since I first began thinking of vocation. What is the role of a layperson in caring for the sick and the hungry and the poor? What is the role of an ordained priest in caring for others, and how is it different from that of a layperson?

Jesus wasn't speaking only to the Pharisees when he declared in answer to their question, "Love the Lord your God with all your heart and with all your soul and with all your mind. . . . [And] love your neighbor as yourself" (Matt. 22:37, 39). Jesus was speaking to all of us, no matter our role in society: Love God. Love yourself. Love your neighbors.

As an ordained priest, Tom nourished Florence that day by bringing his Communion kit, offering his prayers, and wearing his collar—all ways of representing God and the church to her. As a dedicated layperson, I nourished Florence by bringing sacks of groceries, offering words of compassion and friendship, and representing God through our community's love for her. On that day, I knew I was in the proper place, in the right role. I didn't know the answers about my future vocation, but I trusted that my vocation at that moment was God-given.

Delivering groceries was literally part of my job description at the time, but many of us feed others simply because it is our calling as Christ-bearers: the chicken dishes for the parents of a newborn, the pots of soup for the sick neighbor, the pizza dinner for the new family in our church. When we feed one another, we remind ourselves of the power of food and its role in sustaining life. We share God's love in a way that is familiar and accessible. Dramatic as it may sound, we are living out our vocation, Christ in us.

"Eat and you shall be satisfied," Jesus said. When I carry a casserole to a neighbor, I am saying, "Your life matters to me. I want you to live, and I want you to eat and be satisfied."

Were the ways in which Tom and I presented God to a dying woman so different from each other? I believe those bags of groceries, offered with God's love and blessings, were as much the Eucharist for Florence and her family as the consecrated bread and wine were for Tom and me at church on Sunday. For most of the people I encountered through my work, sacks of food were the only sacramental offering they received.

I don't know how Florence would have responded to Tom's offer of Eucharist—he never suggested it to her—but perhaps, on that day, the groceries in those brown paper bags were the body and blood of our Lord Jesus Christ feeding her soul and nourishing her family. Perhaps they were the things she needed most of all.

Chapter
FIVE

ONE
of
US

Hospitality is not to change people,
but to offer them space where change can take place.
—HENRI J. M. NOUWEN

A POPULAR SONG ASKS, "WHAT IF GOD WAS ONE of us?" It has a catchy tune and an upbeat sound, but if you consider the words seriously, it is a thought-provoking query. What if God comes to us in unexpected ways when we don't feel ready? In unexpected places that are not "appropriate"? What if God sits in the middle of the rough and tumble, just waiting for us to find Him?

It is easy for us to sanitize Jesus into someone whom we would want to be friends with, but I don't think that is what the Gospels tell us. They tell us Jesus ate with the lepers and the prostitutes and the tax collectors. He rejected the traditional ways of reaching out to others so He could meet people in the most unexpected places: places of illness, of pain, and of suffering. He meets us in the quiet of an empty sanctuary, in the homes of the dying, in the eyes of a stranger.

I learned this again through an unexpected visitor at church. It was a perfect late-summer day in Sewanee, when the sky turns a marvelous shade of clear blue, a color that portends the arrival of a new academic year and a fresh start. It was Otey's "Kick-Off Sunday"—the day when Episcopal churches try to recruit new people to attend Sunday school and Bible study groups. Everyone was looking ahead and feeling festive and optimistic. Tables dotted the lawn of the rectory, with colorful balloons tied to chairs. It was an abundant gathering of people and food.

When we planned this day at the parish each year, we wanted new people to come join us, to share in the joy of our community and our ministries. But having a true stranger in our midst was not what any of us anticipated.

I don't know exactly what drew Carly to our parish on that day, but I suspect she'd seen all the gaiety and decided to stop by. Soon after she arrived, she told those around her that she was a college graduate and that she had just taken an overdose of pills in an unsuccessful effort to kill herself and the baby she was carrying. She was still strung out from the drugs and she was hungry, she said.

She had our attention.

The people of the parish rallied around her. One moved her inside to a comfortable meeting room with a couch.

Another made her a plate of food from the potluck lunch we were about to enjoy. Still another brought her big glasses of ice-cold lemonade and water, bringing both so she could choose. Someone came looking for me, hoping I could do more to help her. Little did they know their hospitality was the essence of the day: the thing we needed to do for Carly was to welcome her as Jesus, as God, as the stranger in our midst.

By the time I reached her, Carly was resting, stretched out on the couch, her plate cleaned and the lemonade glass drained.

Carly expanded her story for me. Her family had kicked her out because of her drug habit. She had lost custody of her first child, a three-year-old son. She was pregnant again with nowhere to turn. Many years ago, she had attended a meeting of Alcoholics Anonymous at the church, she said, which is why she stopped.

She and I talked for several minutes. Her story seemed cohesive, but she kept drifting in and out, and I was trying to assess what was really going on. I asked her how we could help right now. She said she needed a place to stay and money. But when she told me she remembered this room from that AA meeting long ago, I sensed more was going on here.

I stepped outside of the meeting room and found a parishioner who had taught me about Christian hospitality by the example of her own life. I asked her to stay with Carly.

"Carly, I'm not leaving, but I am going to find someone who I think can help us. My friend is going to sit here with you in case you need anything else. Is that OK?" I asked.

"That's fine," she said, looking sleepy again and closing her eyes. My friend nodded and I left the room.

I went and found the parishioner who led AA in our community and brought him into the process. Skillfully and forcefully, he talked to Carly about taking a step toward a new life, toward saving the baby, toward saving her own life. From his decades of experience in leading interventions with people of all ages and backgrounds, this man knew the right words to use with a person overcome by addiction. Carly, however, wanted nothing to do with hospitals or doctors, which was what he recommended.

Carly kept trying to distract us with irrelevant facts. She did not seem interested in the health of her unborn child. We prayed with her, each of us placing our hands on Carly's shoulders as she sat stony and unmoved by any of our words. We weren't getting anywhere. I needed a break to clear my head and make some phone calls to get more professional help.

Much of what Carly was telling us seemed true: the suicidal tendencies (supported by the scars on her wrists), the overdose (which showed in her dilated eyes and her inability to follow conversation sometimes), the hunger (her plate was empty in no time), and the lack of sleep (she would doze off, either from exhaustion or the drugs, each time we left the room). She was clearly in need of medical help. Her pregnancy, however, was hard to confirm—four months is one of those times when some women show and others don't, and she was a large girl. I call her a "girl," but she said she was twenty-eight years old—old enough to be called a woman, though her emotional maturity seemed more like that of a teenager.

I started calling shelters and emergency hotlines. I found no help for Carly. Shelters for battered women don't want drug addicts. Shelters for the homeless don't want mentally ill people. Homes for pregnant women don't want the drugs or the suicidal issues. I went to find a parishioner who was also a physician and asked her advice. She was clear and direct: take her immediately to the emergency room and leave her there for the proper authorities to deal with. It was simple: go to the hospital. But I knew Carly would not go.

I found the parish's brand-new interim priest, Jerrie. I hoped someone with more authority than I, a real priest wearing that collar, could command Carly's respect and attention. I gently drew Jerrie aside and told her of the situation. "Just pray with her," I said. "I don't know what we're going to do, but another voice can't hurt."

I took Jerrie to meet Carly. I went to make more phone calls. Fifteen, maybe twenty, minutes passed. When I went back into the room, I found Jerrie praying with Carly, blessing her and the baby, marking her forehead with the sign of the cross. Jerrie had somehow broken through. During the conversation, Carly revealed that she knew a lot about "the system" in place for people with mental illness, for homeless pregnant women, for the poor. She moved from her cold, withdrawn approach to almost bragging to Jerrie about how smart she was. With a glance between our AA leader and me, Jerrie moved to the "tough love" approach. Before she became a priest, Jerrie had been an attorney, so she knew this role too.

"Carly," Jerrie said, "I may have to report you to the authorities because of what you've told us today. You've endangered the life of your baby, and Laura and I may have to do something about this."

Now Carly became completely engaged and incensed. She bolted up from her slumped position, her eyes became angry and bright, and she waved her hands as she screamed at us all.

"You said I could make my own choice about what happened next and now you are tricking me," she yelled. She ranted about how we were lying about helping her and now we were going to turn her in. The droopy eyes and passive attitude disappeared.

"If that's the case," Carly said, "then I lied to you about the baby. I'm not pregnant. And I didn't take any pills."

Jerrie asked her why she had lied.

"To get your attention," Carly replied.

"You need to go the hospital and make sure you are OK," I said. "We've got food and bread to give you and we'll take you to the ER."

"No, I'll go to a hospital myself," Carly said, "but I'll take the groceries with me."

"Where will you sleep tonight?" Jerrie asked.

"I guess I'll go back to my aunt's," she said.

As we carried her groceries out, I encouraged her to come back for AA meetings or more food. Her car, a fairly new Mercury, was full of revealing things: empty soda cans and chip bags; unopened mail; a tiny children's T-shirt bought at Cracker Barrel, still in the thin plastic bag; a book about depression; a fat paperback reference guide to drugs; and, in the back, a car seat just the right size for a three-year-old.

Was any part of what she had told us true? She clearly had money to buy the little T-shirt. She knew she had a mental illness and had the resources to learn about various medications. She wasn't flat broke if she was subsisting on a diet of soda and chips. She'd had custody of her son recently enough to leave his car seat in her car.

What was true? What was a lie?

Did it matter?

In the end, Carly didn't get much from us other than a huge amount of emotional energy, some heartfelt prayers, a bag of groceries, a plate of tasty food, a glass of cool lemonade, and words of encouragement.

Did we love her? Yes. Did we care for her as best we could? Yes. We did what Jesus called us to do.

I wonder now if one of us should have taken her to the hospital to have her checked out, but it seemed impossible at the time. She would never have gone. She would have fled even faster and angrier than she did.

Still, I worried for a long time about the outcome of the situation. Was there a baby? Where would Carly's next fix (emotional or otherwise) come from? I prayed for Carly and her baby and her young son. I prayed that she found the peace she was looking for, the peace that passes all understanding, the peace that comes from God.

We never saw Carly again. She never came for more groceries. I understand from friends that she didn't attend an AA meeting. I don't know why I expected she might.

Our brief encounter with this stranger led me to ask again: When is Jesus among us? Carly coming to church that day was so unusual, it made it easier to ask that question. But is Jesus also the person who frustrates me when I call about my credit card bill? Is Jesus the person in my office whose every action annoys me for inexplicable reasons? Is Jesus the woman who lives in my building, who I see every day but never stop to ask her name? Is Jesus my former brother-in-law, alcoholic and lost to this world? Is Jesus the once-close friend with whom I haven't spoken in eighteen years?

Is Jesus the people in our life who make us the most anxious, angry, or uncomfortable?

Jesus is each of these people—the ones we love, the ones we hate, the ones we don't even notice. The challenge for me is to remember that Jesus doesn't just show up on Sunday, or in church, or in those blessed bags of groceries. Jesus is in the messiest places of our lives. And Jesus calls us to love those places where He comes to us, even when we don't think we can do it.

Repeatedly, God snaps me out of my narrow view and reminds me that Jesus is in each of these people. Loving them, even in the most ordinary settings, is loving Christ.

On that bright day, like so many others, I felt caught between the laity and the ordained: a bit priest, a bit not, trying to be both in the same skin; trying to have the authority and presence that comes from the trappings of the priesthood yet also seeking to be a caring individual, irrespective of what I wear or who told me I could do this job.

I haven't figured out why some people, such as Carly, respond to a priest, and others, such as Rebecca asking to be baptized on that rainy day, respond to a layperson. Maybe none of us know why we respond to different people. None of us can predict how God will arrive.

But God did come to us on that Sunday at church. God was there in our morning worship. God was there in the meal we shared. God was there in our fellowship and hospitality. God was also there in the ordinary, in the confusion, in the stranger. And it is often in the surprises of God that we find our true calling.

Chapter
SIX

FEED

My

SHEEP

If you judge people, you have no time to love them.
—MOTHER TERESA

A T TIMES IN MY WORK, I KNEW MOMENTS OF great spiritual intimacy and the profound presence of God, such as during Rebecca's baptism, my final visit with Florence, and even the mysterious afternoon with Carly. But at other times, my work seemed too mundane for the presence of God. God's name wasn't stamped on the electric bills I paid or the overdue medical statements I saw. I did an ordinary job with ordinary challenges. The only difference was that it took place at a church.

One particular Thursday morning I drove to work thinking about the day ahead and wondering if I was making any difference. I opened my office at 9:30 a.m. and started meeting with the clients who were patiently lined up in the hallway.

First were a few well-known clients, the regulars who needed bills paid or hadn't gotten food on the usual grocery day. Each person who came in wanted to share a story or concern with me—a part of his or her life.

One told me her second son had been diagnosed with autism and she didn't understand what that meant or how to care for him. Her oldest son was deeply disturbed (he pulled a knife on other children at a ten-year-old's birthday party), and he demanded most of her time and attention. Unlike mothers of autistic children in my middle-class world, she didn't care what caused autism. She didn't want to talk about vaccines or macrobiotic diets or homeschooling. She wasn't looking to point a finger or assign blame; she was merely grateful to have a diagnosis that helped her understand her withdrawn child. In her life, he was not the most difficult child, so labeling him autistic was a blessing of a diagnosis, as she called it. The older son had already been hospitalized, and his psychiatric problems were overwhelming to her. We barely even talked about him that day. I encouraged her to find out more about autism through her nurse practitioner and to ask her social worker about resources to help the boy. I paid half of her electric bill and half of her mother's electric bill (her mother had accompanied her on this visit) and then sent them off with big bags of groceries along with encouragement about a diagnosis that clarified the mystery of her quiet, reserved boy.

One by one, people moved through the office, each with a story to tell. There'd been an attempted murder in a remote cove to discuss, and the weather had been brutally hot. One woman had made a successful visit to a generous local dentist who fixed her broken front tooth. She grinned broadly to show off her new smile. A missing front tooth had been a daily reminder of her poverty and had made her feel embarrassed and ashamed. Now she no longer spoke with her hand in front of her mouth.

Each person would have stayed all morning to visit, but a line filled the hallway. They knew the routine: if no one was waiting, they could stay as long as they liked, shooting the breeze and chatting about what was going on in town. If people were waiting, though, everyone moved along to the same rhythm—describe what was going on, see if help was available, get a bag of groceries, and make space for the next person.

I had heard about Karin before I met her, so when she came to my office, I already knew her story. I realized, however, that it was important for her to tell it, so I sat and listened, asking questions to keep her focused when she strayed too far from the facts.

Karin looked just as she'd been described to me: waiflike, with limp blonde hair and very thin. She was neatly dressed and clean, though, with a kind smile and large blue eyes clouded by exhaustion, one of her eyes drifting to the side as she talked. A mutual friend had told me that Karin was leaving an abusive husband, so I expected her to be scared and timid.

But I didn't expect her to be starving—literally starving.

A group of college students had packed groceries the day before, so more than thirty brown paper sacks, filled to the top, sat on the floor of my office. Karin had to step around the bags to sit down in the folding chair across from my desk. She tried to keep talking to me, but I saw her eyes drawing like magnets to the food so close to her feet.

Her daughter, Hayley, was less subtle. Four years old, dressed head-to-toe in pink, she was hungry, and no measure of toddler manners was going to stop her. This week's bags were especially kid friendly, with treats peeking out the top of every sack.

Hayley began pulling out juice boxes and granola bars, asking her mom, "Can I have this?" "What about this?"

Karin was visibly embarrassed by Hayley's behavior. I assured Karin it was fine for Hayley to have whatever she wanted. Karin's son, eight-year-old James, had been quiet, never making eye contact with me until then.

"Me too?" he asked plaintively.

"Of course," I said. "Anything you see, as long as it's OK with your mom, is fine to eat."

James got up and went to the open shelf where all the miscellaneous items were placed. He picked up a box of chocolate protein bars. He looked at me without saying a word. The hunger on his face asked the implicit question, Can I have these?

Karin and Hayley had been silent behind me, and I didn't realize what was happening until I looked back.

Both of them were eating raspberry Nutri-Grain bars as fast as they could. They had almost finished an entire box when I turned around. Hayley had drained two juice boxes and was struggling with the straw for a third when I reached over to help. Their eyes were focused and dark—I could tell they hadn't eaten in some time.

Karin swallowed her mouthful of food, and with tears welling up in her eyes, started apologizing, "I was just eating what Hayley said she didn't like."

"I know you are hungry. Eat whatever you'd like, whatever tastes good," I said.

Eating the fruit bars seemed to take the edge off her hunger, so we finally talked about what was happening to her and how CAC could help. Karin had never had a place of her own. Getting electricity to a home was one of those life skills I took for granted, but Karin had moved from her father's house to her husband's house, with no need to establish service because someone else had always taken care of it for her. She wasn't unable to do this; she just didn't know what steps to take. I walked her through what to do, where to go, what papers she would need, and how much it would cost. Then I took two bags of groceries as Karin took a child by each hand and I walked her to her car.

As they left my office, I thought: *They will be back. This will not be easy for them.*

The Thursday that I had dreaded as I drove to work became another day I would never forget. The day when I thought I would find nothing but routine paperwork and endless check-writing brought me face-to-face with the reality of God in the faces of the hungry—a reminder that God was in charge of each these lives, not me.

On that day, we fed starving children and a famished mother. I could not solve all their problems, but I offered love and compassion and food. And giving food was the most important thing that day—for them and for me.

I did the thing God placed in front of me that day. I fed the sheep Jesus put in my care. It was the next step.

It was only a few days after Karin and her children hungrily ate that food in my office that I attended a meeting about a low-income housing program in our county. Many good, fine people were there.

As the group considered how the recent recipients of new houses were faring, and how to pick the next family for a new house, I offered observations about different families. I had known most of them for years and was often able to report specifics about their life circumstances.

One of the faithful "church ladies" in the group, with a pointed finger and sharp tone in her voice, said, "Why aren't you helping these people get out of poverty? Some of them have been getting help all their adult lives! After all you've done for some of them, why are they still coming back for more?"

I was so angry I could barely speak. My voice shook when I finally spoke.

"If we could wave a magic wand and solve addiction, mental illness, and the nation's healthcare crisis, we could solve rural poverty," I said slowly, trying not to scream at her.

Then I reminded her of what we could do.

"We are putting tiny bandages of love on gaping societal wounds," I said. "That's all we can do. We feed people, we love them, we offer them a safe place to come and talk, and we share their sorrows. That's it. We cannot fix the education system, get transportation for families, or create jobs for the unemployed. We are not in the business of solving rural poverty. We are in the business of feeding people with love."

What I really wanted to say to the church lady was, "Come walk a day in my shoes. Come hear the stories of abuse, starvation, and brokenness; of psychotic behavior; of lies and deceit; of death and suicide and chronic illness. Then, after a day or a week or a month or a decade in those shoes, maybe you'll figure it out. So far, I haven't."

I tried to temper my anger. Some days I regret I didn't let her have it. Maybe I was too calm, too patient, too placid.

But if I had let my anger about the unfairness I saw every day take over, no one would want to come near me. No one

FINDING GOD IN A BAG OF GROCERIES

wants to know that poverty is never simple. Yes, much of what poor people suffer is preventable—but to overcome poverty it takes money, and life skills, and more money, and transportation, and good doctors, and a roof that doesn't leak, and generous employers, and perseverance, optimism, support, and more money.

Poverty is much more complex than it looks on TV or in the movies. And rural poverty can be nearly invisible. There is no public park bench for the homeless to sleep on, no grate for someone to build a cardboard shelter over, no soup kitchen with a line winding around a city block. Homeless people in small towns sleep in cars and stay warm wandering twenty-four-hour stores; and in Sewanee, they visit CAC for food when they are hungry. Real poverty is complicated, confusing, and uncertain.

And the truth was, as I should have told the church lady, it was a constant battle not to judge or criticize my clients. It was hard to love people who regularly made bad choices and weren't prepared for the consequences. It was hard to remember that one financial setback in my life might be an annoyance to me, but in their lives it was devastating. I had to choose to love even when it didn't fix anything.

But loving them was what I tried to do—every day. And by doing it for those who came to CAC, I learned to do it better for those nearest to me, for those in my family, and even for myself. Because, like my clients, like you, I am poor, too—in even deeper ways than I can understand.

★

What does it feel like to live on the margins of society? I imagine I know because of the petty things that have happened to me: being the last chosen for kickball, being excluded from a party I hoped to be invited to, being passed over for a job I wished for. Those kinds of things leave me wondering if I'm living on the margins, being left behind while everyone else goes to Cinderella's ball.

Then something shakes me from self-centeredness. Maybe it is a piece on the radio about a tragic shooting in a public place or a story in the newspaper about human trafficking. Maybe it is a blog post from a friend who works in Ugandan orphanages or my own Thursday morning with Karin and her starving children. None of my insignificant concerns mean a thing to people who have real problems, who truly live on the real fringes of society.

They are the people who have truly been left out, left behind, left empty. They are invisible to most of us: we may go to the same post office and park our car next to theirs outside the grocery and sit by them in the same waiting room at the doctor's office, yet we don't really see them. Their problems are much greater than who is having a dinner party or whose kids made the basketball team.

Have you ever, in desperation, had to ask someone to pay your bills because otherwise you'd have your lights turned off? Have you ever had to ask for food, lest you and your family go hungry? Have you ever had to choose between filling a prescription and getting a tank of gasoline to get back to the doctor? Have you ever walked into a church outside of your own faith, knowing no one, and asked for someone to pray with you because you had lost all hope?

We want service to others to be pretty and neat, like a cheery Sunday school story. But the stories in the Gospels show us the reality. The blind, the unwashed, the poor—Jesus loved them all. From them, we learn that we, too, are loved. We are not left out.

Many days in my work it was easier to love others in the name of Christ than it was to accept Jesus' unconditional love for me—to realize that I might deserve to be on the outside but that Jesus brings me in.

My clients knew the truth of their need for help more than I did. They waited patiently in the hallway outside my office, often holding something important to them: a bill they hoped we would pay, a child they wanted me to meet, a diagnosis they wanted to tell me about from a recent doctor's visit. They would come with full hands and turn all those things over to us for help, for blessing, for comfort. And they would come with empty hands and let us fill them.

In all my years at the church, I don't know that anything I did eased poverty across our community in the long term. Most days, I wasn't sure we were doing anything except feeding people. But through that simple act of loving those on the fringes, I knew I could be accepted, too. Like everything we do in light of God's love, the giving and receiving of food was God among us.

Chapter
SEVEN

WALKING

into

MYSTERY

When ambition ends, happiness begins.
—THOMAS MERTON

A S THE CHURCH LADY REMINDED ME, ONE OF
the many things I couldn't fix in our community was
others' perceptions of the needy among us. But I did welcome
opportunities to talk about the complications of poverty and
the beauty in loving strangers. I saw educating others about
rural poverty as part of my calling, and I tried to let God do
with my efforts what He would.

Among the talks I gave was one at an annual Greek lead-
ership retreat at the University of the South, the college in
Sewanee. Sometimes these young people were hard to reach.
Most of them had lives of privilege and little frame of reference for true poverty—the kind of poverty that shocked me

on that first visit to Frances and Carter's home; poverty that existed right in their adopted hometown of Sewanee.

These were terrific kids who wanted to make the world a better place. They desired to do the "right thing," and they were poised and knowledgeable. When I started talking about how many people CAC served and all that we provided, their demeanor changed. They could not comprehend what it meant to feed two hundred fifty people in a town of three thousand, when most people they knew were professors or college students, some whose parents were paying the full cost of more than forty thousand dollars a year for them to go to college.

In late August one year, thirty-five college students, all with polished skin and perfect teeth, wearing the latest fashionably casual clothes, gathered on the deep front porch of the former rectory to learn about our ministry. I began by telling them that I used to be just like them. I had wanted to make the world a better place, to make a good living, to be successful. I was an outstanding journalism student because I thought the press was the most important part of our country's democracy. I liked my upper-middle-class upbringing and wanted that for my own children. I imagined myself as an esteemed columnist at a national newspaper or magazine, writing thoughtful pieces that would encourage people to go out and do good.

I didn't plan to do good works myself. Not that I thought I couldn't, but I assumed I'd be better at sharing information in a passionate way to help others do them. I didn't go to college imagining I would have a part-time job serving the poor. In fact, all the things I wanted as a young person—influence, prestige, job security, a fat paycheck, control, and power—were absent from the work I was doing in my community, absent from my life.

The students nodded their heads, but I suspect they thought, *If she really wanted to be a successful journalist, what is she doing in Sewanee, Tennessee, working in a church?* I told them about my journey from their age to my late forties: how I went from journalism, to grant writing to founding an environmental group, then back to fund-raising, and then walking away from those careers; how I embraced a calling to serve my community and use those skills of communication and persuasion to help those around me in need; how I was not earning enough money to support my family on my own, but I had the financial security of my husband's job and a generous extended family.

The students looked shocked when I spoke so openly about something so personal as money—maybe because I was shocked, too.

At lunch, when they settled down with their sodas and box lunches, I dropped the abstractions and told them stories of real people in poverty, people who didn't choose this life for themselves or their families but lived it nonetheless: mothers who lost children to drug and alcohol addictions, grandparents who raised their grandchildren (or even great-grandchildren) because of accidents and tragedies, parents raising their mentally challenged adult children who never had the opportunity for special education classes.

One student began to cry as I told the story of a longtime client, a lovely older woman named Nell, who was retired from working at the hospital and often came in for groceries and conversation. Nell arrived at my office a day after someone had donated their extra dishes to us. We were planning to hold them until a family lost their home in a fire and needed them. The donated dishes looked to be a mostly complete service for six of a traditional Pfaltzgraff pattern—ivory with blue flowers in the center of the plate—including all the bowls, plates, serving pieces, cups, and saucers.

"Can I have these dishes, Miss Laura?" Nell asked, gently stroking one of the cups. Nell would ask for anything that wasn't nailed down in the office, and I often was frustrated with her for wanting everything for herself. If she saw it, she asked about it.

"Nell, these were just donated so we can give them to a family who gets burned out. I am going to save them with the other things we have for emergencies," I said.

"If that's the case, can I bring you my dishes and trade them for these?" Nell asked. I was impressed with her ingenuity. "I've never had matched dishes before," she admitted.

This is when the college student looked at her lap and began wiping her eyes. We all came from homes where we took matched dishes for granted. Most of us lived in homes where we had multiple matched sets, maybe even a special set for Christmastime.

I gave Nell an empty box to take home with her.

"Bring this back with your dishes and I'll trade you," I said. "I'll save these for you."

Nell returned the next day with a box of assorted dinner plates and bowls. All of them were clean, but not two of them went together. We carefully packed the Pfaltzgraff into another box for her to take home.

This story has a happy ending. A few months after this, Nell came in, beaming and bubbling with a story to tell me.

"I wish you could have seen my Thanksgiving table, Miss Laura," she said. "It was so beautiful with all the dishes on it. My sons and their families thought it was so nice. It made us very thankful."

It was the story about matched dishes on a dinner table that got the students engaged. The stories of drugs and sickness and death didn't speak to them as deeply as a simple story about something that represents safety and haven and home. It made real the people we served: a woman trying to live on a pittance plus tips earned at the local Waffle House; another trying to go to community college while managing her serious mental illness; a dad having to decide whether to pay the electric bill or get groceries to feed his children. It wasn't neat and tidy to explain, and I didn't want to minimize any single person's situation. But sharing those stories showed the college students that poverty is all around us. We cannot ignore it. And we cannot forget that hospitality to one person makes a difference.

By this point in the day, I was tired of talking and they were tired of confronting so many ideas at once. So, we packed groceries together. We did something tangible.

Working in teams, we filled seventy-five paper grocery bags with peanut butter, soup, green beans, corn, macaroni and cheese, pears, spaghetti sauce and pasta, kidney beans, pinto beans, rice, granola bars, ramen noodles, and bags of M&Ms. We did something together to do good. We did it because we needed a break from the sadness of these situations, not to diminish them, but to recognize them and feel we could respond.

The students would be back, sometimes alone or sometimes with a big group of friends, and we would pack groceries again and again. No more talking or thinking was necessary because we had found a way to take steps to alleviate poverty and suffering right in our own community. For a few of those students, this was simply a way to fulfill a service requirement. For others, it was part of a class on "food and hunger" or "the politics of poverty."

For others, it was simply an opportunity to do good, just as they had planned at the beginning of the day. For most of us, though, it was a way to see God in one another, to learn that God appears to us in mysterious and unexpected ways and we are called to respond.

Chapter
EIGHT

HOLY

Listening

God's first language is silence.
—SAINT JOHN OF THE CROSS

THE FOLLOWING WEEK I WAS BACK IN THE office and saw a stream of clients. Everyone was eager to tell me their stories.

Melody came to tell me her husband had pneumonia that had caused him to miss more than two weeks of work. He was so sick that she stayed home with him, missing her own work. People like Melody and her husband don't have paid sick leave. He's a carpenter and she's a teacher's aide at a small preschool, so when they don't work, they don't get paid. Once he gets healthy and they start working again, things will be better. For the moment, I paid half of her electric bill and gave her two bags of groceries, hoping the additional food would help.

Then Leland came in. His situation had gotten worse. I'd known Leland since my first day at CAC, and he taught me a hard lesson.

Leland had first arrived at my office when I was still figuring out how to use the telephone and find the files. He was near tears. He was about to lose his home, a trailer house, unless he made a $750 payment that day to catch up what he owed, which was two months of back payments. He, his wife, and their two young children would be homeless tonight if we didn't do something immediately. He had waited until the last minute to ask for help and now it was a crisis. Rather, it was his crisis that I let become my crisis.

Pixie, the CAC board chairwoman, had come into the office to help me on my first day. It was a great gift that she was there. I had no idea what to do for Leland. At that point, we never helped anyone with more than $100 toward any bill, but I couldn't bear the idea of those children being evicted right after Christmas. The weather was cold and icy, as winters in Sewanee can be.

Pixie and I agreed we should help the family, making an exception to our maximum assistance rules because of the circumstances. Because Leland didn't have reliable transportation, Pixie drove the money to the lender, about forty-five miles away. And Leland went to his home with three bags of groceries. I felt as if I had done something really valuable that day, patting myself on the back.

About six months later, Leland came back needing help with his electric bill. I noticed that the address on the bill was not the same as the address of the trailer we'd paid $750 to keep.

"What's going on with this different address?" I asked.

"We lost the trailer to the bank," he said sheepishly.

He didn't say, "I'm so sorry." Or, "I should have told you." He just said they'd lost it. No explanation.

I felt sick as I wrote the check for half of his electric bill, which was probably less than $50. I felt used. The money we'd given him was like money we'd shoved down a rat hole. I hadn't made it a loan (because I knew he could not pay it back), but now it was gone with no chance of seeing it again. It would have paid ten electric bills or bought a truckload of food, and it was all gone.

Now Leland was back, as he had been many times since I started at CAC, and he needed something simple. His young boys wanted to play soccer in the town league but he couldn't afford the registration fees. I told him I'd work it out with the soccer league board; we made scholarships that year for about half a dozen kids.

The procession of needs continued in the office all day.

"They cut part of my heel off," said the diabetic Vietnam veteran. "I limp but I don't want anyone to know how bad it is. I still need to work, even though it hurts so much."

"I got all my teeth pulled out at the traveling medical clinic. They were too rotted to leave in and the infection was going to kill me. I've got to wait at least six months before I can get false teeth. I don't know how I'll pay for them," said the finest caregiver to Sewanee's well-off, elderly folks.

"My daughter's having a baby. She's got a bifurcated uterus so she's having a hard time and is in a lot of pain. The boy who knocked her up won't do anything to help," the girl's abusive alcoholic mother told me.

"My grandson gave an old man a ride into town. After he dropped him off, the police pulled him over for a bum taillight. The old guy had left his stash [of marijuana] on the seat and my boy got busted. He was set up," said one man.

"My husband's been stealing my Xanax and taking them. He's an addict. I've got a lock box of my own now so he can't take my drugs," said a woman who told me she was trying to stay clean.

"You know that girl who was just in here? Don't believe a word of what she said. She's the one who's stealing Xanax and selling it all over town," said her neighbor who came next into my office.

"My nephew keeps trying to kill himself, and his momma doesn't want to mess with him anymore so she lets him go to school all cut up. She's just hoping that DCS [Department of Children's Services] takes him away and puts him in a hospital. She's an awful mother and he don't deserve to live like that," said the worried aunt with hair the color of an eggplant.

"Me and my wife are going on a cruise in February and everyone's mad at us about it, saying we're taking food from the hungry by coming up here. But it was a gift, Laura, from our kids, and we couldn't say no. I wanted you to know the truth. We still need help. But we are going to Mexico on the trip—it might be the only time my wife gets to do this. She'll begin her chemo when we get back," said my client who also happened to drive a used Volvo.

"I've written a song for the president, Ms. Willis. You know the way to Washington, don't you? Will you drive me there? When he hears this, he's going to want me to come sing at the White House. I've put it up on YouTube and sent him a letter. Here, let me sing it for you," said a woman about my age who was brilliant but struggled with bipolar disorder. She wouldn't take her medications regularly, so she couldn't hold down a job.

"My boy won't go to school anymore. He was on the playground and these boys circled around him and started teasing him. Then they tackled him and pulled his pants down to his ankles and knocked him over. He was so humiliated, Ms. Willis. I don't blame him for not wanting to go back. And the principal says there's nothing she can do about it. 'Boys will be boys,' she said, but I think he's scared and I don't blame him," said one woman.

My most frequent response that day, and every day I sat behind that desk, was, "Is there anything we can do to help?" or "Can we pray about this?"

But silently, I asked, *Where is God in this? How could God watch this march of poverty and sadness and indifference and need and not intervene?* I couldn't change their lives. Most of the time, I can't change my own life. I couldn't tell my clients that things would get easier, illnesses would be healed, or debts would be paid. All I could say was that there are many things we simply don't understand. All I could tell them was that they were loved, that someone cared enough to help, to offer a bag of groceries, and that they were not alone. I could carry some of their pain, ease their burden, if only for a few minutes.

Knowing the pain and sadness of their families' lives helped me recognize those same things in my life—the things I wouldn't be honest about, either, unless I was in sacred space, with someone I could trust. I could try to be for them the face of Jesus that I wished to see in my own life, just as they were Jesus for me.

By the time I went home on a day like that, I felt like a beloved, well-used vessel that the Holy Spirit had rushed through like water all day. The vessel is suited to the task, but it is worn when the day ends. It is still whole, but a minuscule part of its pottery has eroded away from use.

I was not fully expended. I was still eager to go home to my family and care for them and let them care for me. But after serving as host for this movement of light and grace, I was tired. Deeply tired. And so very sad by the things I saw and the words I heard and the lives I shared.

Real ministry for me required an emptying of myself hour after hour, day after day. It never made me feel good or special or saintly. Maybe that is why there are specific words in the Episcopal prayer book to encourage this work:

> [Let us pray] for all who are in danger, sorrow, or any kind of trouble;
> *For those who minister to the sick, the friendless, and the needy.*[1]

After a day that stretched my imagination, my compassion, and my heart, I felt more broken than ever, and I knew others were more broken than I could ever see.

And so I am beginning to learn that God does not call us to "fix" things through our vocation. God calls us to live our vocation. One of the ways I have discovered this truth, and continue to absorb it, is through contemplative prayer.

Just before I started at CAC, I was introduced to the practice of contemplative prayer as I struggled to connect my vocation with my faith. This ancient form of silent prayer is a way of communicating with God by allowing God to speak to us, rather than our speaking to God. Some have described it as a way we experience God's presence within us, "closer than breathing, closer than thinking, closer than consciousness itself."[2] This form of prayer is both a relationship with God and a discipline to foster that relationship.

When I was first invited to participate in a daylong contemplative (read: silent) retreat, I laughed. Loudly. A natural extrovert, I have a hard time remaining quiet in a committee meeting. I was certain I could not spend a day without speaking. A friend active in the contemplative prayer movement was persuasive, however, and said, "Come try it. What do you have to lose?"

A day in complete silence. I thought, *What a terrible, scary thing.* I could not imagine being quiet for even twenty minutes. What would I find out about myself and about my relationship with God? What if there was nothing there?

But I decided if God wanted to come to me through silence, I was willing to try.

On that first day, I spent the first two twenty-minute periods of silence trying to keep from hyperventilating. Every part of my body wanted to squirm. My nose itched. My foot wiggled. I fidgeted in my chair. During the day's third sit (the shorthand way of describing each twenty-minute period of prayer), my body calmed and my brain settled. I breathed slowly and deeply. I was still. I was quiet. I was open to God. Grace happened.

A day of experiencing the peace of quiet grew to a daily practice of sitting erect, eyes closed, clearing my mind of thoughts and concerns, for twenty minutes. Twice a day was great; once was often all I could fit in. The longer I practiced

the discipline, the easier it became to adapt to the silence. I didn't see that I was growing any closer to God, but my family knew something was changing. When I became short-tempered or irritable, one of the men in my life would tell me, "You need a sit!"

My daily practice grew into leading a weekly group where we prayed in silence together, attending numerous eight-day silent retreats, and a life enriched by this prayer. With the silence came a deeper compassion for others, a greater understanding of how service and silence fit together, and a realization of how I could learn so much more by being quiet.

Only by looking back do I realize how God used silent prayer to prepare me for my ministry at CAC: to be quiet and listen carefully, to love deeply, and to recognize that God was in charge of all things. The problems of the world were not mine to solve.

As the intensity of my work at CAC grew, so did my need for this quiet time of prayer each day. Added to my weekly Eucharist and worship with my family at Otey Parish, my spiritual life was full. The three things became so intertwined, I wasn't sure where one stopped and the other began: prayer—loving others through service—prayer—Holy Eucharist—prayer—compassion—prayer—Holy Eucharist. My contemplative prayer practice fed my ministry, which was fed by my trip to the Communion table, which was fed by my caring for the poor.

When I was frustrated by my inability to transform the

lives of all the people in need that I met, I turned to silent prayer. When I was mad at poverty and the politics behind it, I turned to silent prayer. When I struggled with the comment made to me so often, "You should be a priest," I turned to silent prayer.

Prayer helped me shed my anger and confusion and helplessness. During those twenty-minute times of quiet, I imagined myself resting in God's great hands, where I was safe and cared for, and God was in control.

Contemplative prayer reminds us that if we don't have the answers to our questions about vocation, maybe we should be quiet and listen—listen to our intuition; listen to our heart; listen to God. And when we see we aren't getting answers to the questions we are asking, we might need to ask different questions. The silence helps us be content with no answers at all. It helps us see that above all, we need God's grace.

Because although it might be easier to divide service and poverty into "us" and "them," into people with abundant resources and people with little, the people in need are really you and me. We are as helpless as anyone with a hungry belly, as helpless as anyone desperate for a job, as anyone trying to overcome the same addiction again and again. Our common neediness stems from our longing for the good news of God's kingdom, our yearning to be free from sin, and our need for the unconditional love of Jesus Christ.

The stranger and the starving and the hurting remind us: we all hunger for God.

Chapter
NINE

THE

Kingdom of

GOD

The future starts today, not tomorrow.
—POPE JOHN PAUL II

ONE OF THE GREAT JOYS OF MINISTERING IN my community was working with and learning from children about following God's call and serving others. Kids don't overanalyze, project into the future, or become paralyzed because they can't do enough. They do what they can.

In the early fall one year, Alice Phillips's sixth-grade class at Sewanee Elementary School was reading a book about young people making a difference. In one true story, a boy was repairing old bicycles and making them like new for children in foster homes and orphanages. In another, a girl volunteered in her city's homeless shelter preparing meals for the residents. Mrs. Phillips invited her students to think of a project they might like to do in our community and asked me to come talk with them.

Most of the children in this sixth-grade class already knew about my work. For years, CAC had done projects with various groups at the elementary school, as well as schoolwide food drives. One third-grade teacher regularly had her classes come over and pack groceries when they studied communities. Many of the children had packed boxes in Sunday school, or in Scouts, or with their families on a parishwide workday. Proximity helped. With the church located across the street from the elementary school, it was an easy way for the schoolchildren to do community service without a bus ride or a long walk.

Other kids knew about CAC because we provided services to their family: they had seen our blue-and-white logo on a brochure at the bottom of a grocery bag in their home or they had eaten from in a generic can of Beanee Weenees.

When I arrived in Mrs. Phillips's classroom that fall day, I expected it to go something like this: I would describe how difficult it is to ask for help from someone. I would engage the class in talking about food and hunger globally and in our community. With my guidance, we would figure out what they might do as a group. I was planning on them coming over to pack grocery bags together—a necessary part of our work but a fairly simple and routine task many had done before.

Here's the thing about eleven- and twelve-year-olds: they are smarter than you think. I began to realize this as they started telling me what they had in mind as a service project.

The students came up with an ambitious plan for a single day. They wanted to host a special community breakfast on a Wednesday a few weeks out. They wanted to plan the menu, cook the food, set up the tables and chairs, and order the groceries to give away. During the breakfast, they wanted to put on a variety show, with singers, acrobats, and twirlers. I couldn't believe what I was hearing from these young people. They already had a clear vision of what they wanted to accomplish and how to make it happen.

I simply had to get out of the way. And I did.

The sixth-graders made and distributed flyers describing the event. They wrote news articles for the local weekly newspaper and the county biweekly newspaper. They collected and decorated cardboard boxes for food. We made a shopping list and chose a balanced selection of items to put in the food boxes.

As we talked, they wondered if we could get fresh fruit for the clients. I explained that through the food bank, we could normally get only canned, nonperishable items.

"But we want them to have fresh things, too," one girl said. So I ordered cases of apples and oranges from the local grocer. Class members decorated little paper shopping bags to serve as "fruit baskets."

Closer to the event, they unloaded the truck filled with more than one thousand pounds of food: cases of peanut butter, macaroni and cheese, canned chili, pasta, tuna fish, soup, cold cereal, juice boxes, spaghetti sauce, green beans, applesauce, and saltine crackers.

As the day approached, I met with them again in their classroom. I had them each call out what they wanted to cook or what they liked best for breakfast. We soon had a whiteboard covered with ideas for our meal. They thought of every possible breakfast item—everything from biscuits and gravy to huevos rancheros to Pop-Tarts and beef jerky. If you had been watching this happen, you could tell who ate breakfast supervised by an adult and who was left to scavenge for breakfast on their own. The kids who suggested fresh-fruit smoothies and eggs Benedict lived very different lives from the kids who suggested peanut butter and jelly sandwiches, but they all offered something to the board.

We started eliminating items. We don't have enough blenders for smoothies; beef jerky isn't a good breakfast option unless you are camping; fried eggs are too time-consuming for a crowd; hollandaise sauce is too complicated. We whittled down the list on the board to a manageable meal they could prepare: scrambled eggs, bacon, pancakes, cut-up fresh fruit, muffins donated by the local coffee shop, coffee, juice, and milk.

I still wasn't sure how we could accomplish all their lofty goals. How could we get everyone to work together, to offer generous hospitality and compassionate respect, all the while not setting the parish hall on fire? Four main tasks had to be accomplished that morning at about the same time: cook, greet, serve, and carry out groceries.

Mrs. Phillips generously gave her class over to me for an hour or two a week as we plodded through the details of the event. If you've ever planned a big dinner party or a reception, you can understand that planning it *with* twenty-two kids, rather than *for* them, is a challenge. And they viewed this as their project, not my project or Mrs. Phillips's project or anyone else's. They wanted to be in charge and do the work.

In the closing days before the event, I gave them a bit of a lecture, which was a departure from the free-for-all conversations we'd had over the past weeks.

"I need each of you to look inside yourself, evaluate your talents and gifts, and write on this index card what you really want to do on this day," I said to them, very solemnly, passing out the cards. "I don't want you to think about what your best friend is going to do, because his or her gifts are not yours. I need each of you to find your best strength and put it to use on this day. Honor what your heart tells you, not what you think everyone else is doing. Don't be bound by what you think you should do. Boys can be cooks; girls can carry out groceries. Listen to your heart." I asked them to list their top three choices of jobs for the day.

Some of them looked confused, their faces squished and worried. Others looked at those index cards with a quiet seriousness. A few wrote immediately from the choices we'd listed on the board. We had talked about the personal qualities it took to do each job. A cook had to be detail-oriented, able to follow instructions, have confidence (although not necessarily experience) in the kitchen, and work safely on his or her own. A greeter had be outgoing and cheerful, welcoming to all, and have the maturity to talk to adults. Greeters also had to have nice handwriting, as they made name tags for everyone. A server had to be exceedingly polite, a good listener, have a friendly face and an open heart, and have great attention to detail. The grocery helpers needed to be strong, able to be responsible in the parking lot, courteous and patient while walking with clients, and independent.

"Finally," I said to them, "if you want to be a leader of the team you are on, please indicate that at the bottom of the card. Leaders must be able to help their team accomplish its goals, and I will look to you leaders during the event if I need your team to do something."

This part of the process was a surprise to them, but I'd watched these boys and girls over the past few weeks and I knew there were natural leaders in this class who never got a chance to be in charge. Small towns and small schools often do this to children: early on, everyone decides Jane is the pretty one, Sam is the smart one, and Jack is the class leader. I knew from this group that there were some kids who wanted to be leaders but would never get elected class president or selected as team captain without this chance.

They turned in their cards to me and I took them home to ponder their requests. Some of them were very simple: name, job preferences, and nothing else. Some of them were extravagantly decorated with appeals: "Please, Mrs. Willis, all I want to be is a server! Please!" one said, with daisies drawn all over the card. Others were simple but clear: "I want to be a leader. I've never been one before so I want to try it."

I tried to give everyone their first choice, although I had to move a few people around to even out the teams. I selected team leaders from the students who expressed an interest but weren't known as class leaders. I ran the list past Mrs. Phillips before we told the children their jobs.

"Laura, this is amazing. I would never have thought that Chris wanted to be a leader, but I think he can do it," she said. We both agreed that another child could not be paired with her best friend because they would get too easily distracted, so we split them up. For the most part, though, the kids self-selected themselves into just the right organization.

In the final days before the breakfast, we announced the team groupings to them. They gathered, one team in each corner of the classroom, and had the most amazing, mature conversations. Without prompting, the cooks wanted to know if I would provide aprons for them or did they need to bring their own. The servers wanted to know if I could get real order pads for them, and they decided to all wear purple shirts on the day of the event. The greeters talked about how they would make pretty name tags for guests, and how they would station two greeters at each set of doors in the building. The helpers figured out they, too, needed to dress alike, and they settled on white shirts. The leaders helped their teams work together to think about the logistics, and as Mrs. Phillips and I eavesdropped on each group, we were stunned at their complex planning. They were taking responsibility for things I hadn't even thought about.

I recruited four parents to help on the morning of the event. One family donated from their farm dozens of fresh eggs to be scrambled. The servers decided they wanted to decorate the tables, so they made fall flower and leaf arrangements of things they found in the yard and the woods nearby.

Just a week before the breakfast, one of the children in the class, Russell, pulled me aside. Russell's mother was a long-time client of the CAC and normally came to the breakfasts we hosted with the help of adult volunteers. His situation concerned me, but I thought I'd let him take the lead and not say anything until I had to.

"Mrs. Willis, I think my mom and uncle are going to come to breakfast," he said quietly. "Is that OK?"

"Of course it is, Russell, if it is OK with you. Have y'all talked about it?" I said.

"Yes. I think it is OK."

"It is entirely up to you, Russell, how you interact with her. Some people may know she's your mom and others may not. There's nothing to be embarrassed of—you know she works hard to provide for you. I'm just glad it is OK with you that she comes. It will be fine," I reassured him. His mom worked at a diner on the interstate, making $2.13 an hour plus tips, which were negligible.

I had known Russell for several years. As he grew older, he was becoming more aware of how different he was from his affluent classmates. Three years before this breakfast, I was chaperoning a field trip with these same children as third-graders. We were hiking on one of Sewanee's most beautiful trails through Shakerag Hollow. While we were coming up the path toward the bus, Russell ran up to me from the end of the row of hikers, calling out loudly as he passed all the other children, "Mrs. Willis, Mrs. Willis!"

I stopped and looked around, thinking something must be wrong—a child down, a sprained ankle, a shoving incident at the end of the line.

Russell ran up to me and, in front of all the children who had gathered around wondering why he was shouting and breathing hard, said, "Mrs. Willis, my mom wanted me to ask you to leave us some groceries out today. We're out of food and I'm hungry. Can you do that?"

"Yes, Russell," I said, sighing a deep sigh. It was a sigh of relief that the children on the path were OK, but it was also a sigh of sadness and pain for this little boy who, midhike, must have felt his belly rumbling and remembered he needed to ask me for groceries. It seemed not to matter to him that everyone in the class heard him ask for food. He never pulled me aside or whispered his request in my ear. It was just his voice, shouting, "Mrs. Willis! Mrs. Willis!" in that God-blessed space of natural beauty and wonder. In the midst of the Dutchmen's Breeches and rare red trilliums was a child who was hungry. And it didn't matter where we were.

Russell's maturity in asking me quietly now, three years later, about his mother attending the breakfast showed me how much all these children had changed. They were on the cusp of adolescence, that time of dividing up by class and beauty and talent and wealth. Russell knew he might face a life of poverty and need and emptiness.

By all measures, the breakfast hosted by Mrs. Phillips's sixth-grade class was a huge success. The easiest indicator was that many guests came to share the meal, got groceries and fruit, and enjoyed the event. By the end of the morning, all the cooked breakfast was gone and all the groceries and fruit bags had been given away. Everyone ate a delicious hot breakfast and none of our cooks had any injuries. All the orders were taken politely by the wait staff. All the guests and helpers had handmade name tags. No guests carried their own groceries to their car, unless they absolutely insisted.

The normally shy children stepped outside of their comfort zones and were smiling and friendly to strangers. The normally bossy kids let the assigned leaders take charge of their groups. The normally boisterous and disruptive ones were energetic and exuberant but not a problem. Everyone stretched to a new place for this special day.

Breakfast lasted only about ninety minutes, including the entertainment. It seemed as if it had just started and then it was over. Throughout the event, however, many of the children asked, "Mrs. Willis, can we eat?" I kept reminding them that we were serving breakfast, not eating breakfast. "If there is food left," I said, "we'll have some."

During the planning, the children often asked me, "What if we run out of food?" That question, coming up again and again, showed me that the kids understood the deep nature of what we were doing. It would be no gift, no special event, if someone came for breakfast and there was nothing to eat. I would respond each time, "There's always enough food. In all the times I've had these breakfasts, we've never run out."

Early in our conversations in the classroom, I told them the story of Jesus feeding the five thousand, the miracle of the five loaves and two fish that is described in the Gospels: how the disciples were afraid of not being able to feed the crowd and would have preferred to send them away; how Jesus blessed the bread and fish and told the disciples to distribute it; how there were still pieces left over after all were fed. I told them we would not have five thousand people, but we had to trust that there would be enough food. Whether the children had a Christian background or not, I knew they could relate to the great simplicity of this story.

After the last dirty plate was cleared from the table and the last grocery bag taken out to the car, we took a break. Indeed, we did have food left. As the kids were finishing their jobs, Mrs. Phillips and the parent volunteers and I quickly scrambled another few dozen eggs, made a few pancakes, and poured juice. And in a nice turnabout, the kids took off their aprons and their name tags, and the adults served them. They regrouped with their friends and talked about their experiences, or whatever kids talk about as they eat. After they finished, I asked them to think quietly about what they'd just experienced and to reflect on it, either privately or with the group. I posed a series of questions to them:

"How do you feel after today's breakfast? How did you feel greeting people you didn't know? What do you think about what we did together today? Did you have any interesting conversations? Did you have anything awkward or challenging to deal with? What unexpected thing did you learn today? What will you take home from this experience?"

Again, they surprised me with the depth of their insights and their understanding of what they did:

"I felt really good helping people who were hungry."
"The people I waited on were so nice."
"I liked greeting everyone at the door."
"They seemed happy to be here."

"When I carried groceries out, I was surprised by some of
  their cars—they were really old."
"Everyone was polite and said thank you."

No matter how often people came to special events such as
this breakfast, each occasion changed lives. Whether it was
with insightful sixth-graders or college students or community volunteers, these gatherings of disparate people sharing
a meal were the table fellowship that Jesus encouraged
through his life and actions.

When Jesus ate with tax collectors or lepers or women, he
was showing us that the kingdom of God knows no bound-
aries. Heaven is a table where we can all sit together: rich and
poor, men and women, schoolchildren and adults. At its best
moments, that is what ministry is—God among us and
within us, a glimpse of heaven. And on that morning of the
schoolchildren's breakfast, it was heaven indeed.

Chapter
TEN

WOUNDS

of

LOVE

The truth does not change according to our
ability to stomach it.
—FLANNERY O'CONNOR

WOUNDS

of

LOVE

The truth does not change according to our
ability to stomach it.
—FLANNERY O'CONNOR

I N EVERY RELATIONSHIP I HAD WITH PEOPLE IN
my work, I realized I saw into their lives through only one
portal, yet they lived in a very big space with many secret
rooms, sometimes rooms that had been untouched for decades.
So I trod lightly when families tried to draw me into their dis-
agreements. In particular, when I encountered messy situations
between parents and children, I tried to remember that I could
never know what had transpired before I became involved.

But there were a few situations when I felt God draw me
into these families for a reason. In one case, it was to offer
God's love to a young woman who lived in a family with virtually no love at all.

Gwen called to tell me that her seventeen-year-old daughter was cutting herself again, and she didn't know what to do about it.

"Is she seeing a therapist or someone she can talk to about this?" I asked.

"No," Gwen said bitterly. "We can't pay for nothing like that. She just needs to stop. Stupid girl, she's so lazy."

"Oh, Gwen. I know this is scary for you, but Autumn isn't lazy; she just needs help. What she's doing is hurting herself and everyone around her. Let's make an appointment for her to see Dr. Ames and have them talk."

"I don't think that will help. She don't listen to me; she's not going listen to anybody."

"It's worth a try. TennCare [the state's health-care program for low-income families] will cover her appointments, so it won't cost you anything. Will you call Dr. Ames?"

"Maybe."

"Please, Gwen. For yourself and for Autumn and all of your family, call Dr. Ames."

"Are you going to be in the office all day?"

"Yes," I said. "I'll be at the church all day. Would you like to come by and get some groceries?"

"We're out of food. I'll bring Autumn with me. Maybe you can talk some sense into her."

At this point, I couldn't tell her not to come in and not to bring Autumn to me for some kind of pseudocounseling, but I thought if I saw them, maybe I could help assess the seriousness of their situation. I did want to see Autumn myself and make sure she wasn't in danger. And they needed food. I could help.

Gwen had a history of mental illness, and during other visits I had witnessed her being truly hateful to her daughter, a troubled young woman stuck in a home with parents who were sick in so many ways.

In my earliest meetings with Gwen, I learned she took no medication for her mental illness, but I suspected she was addicted to painkillers, which made her mood swings impossible to predict. Autumn, who was a senior in high school, was overweight and already showing the physical scars from her self-inflicted abuse. I couldn't see, and didn't want to know, what scars she might have had from other abuse in the home. I never met her father, Gwen's husband, and no one ever mentioned him though he lived in the same house. This worried me a lot.

Gwen calling her daughter "lazy" was more than the normal mother-daughter frustration. Gwen expected Autumn to do everything at their home: cook and clean, as well as go to school, run errands for her parents, and receive no love in return. It was a wonder she hadn't run away.

My first encounters with Gwen were all by phone. She would call me to curse and rant about what a terrible daughter Autumn was and how she never did anything to help her two ailing parents. During each of these phone calls, I would remind Gwen that Autumn was an excellent student, doing her schoolwork and making good grades, staying out of trouble, and coming home each day. No amount of rational explanation for Autumn's behavior would change Gwen's tirades against her daughter. Gwen's greatest complaint was Autumn's housekeeping.

"Can you find someone to come clean our house?" Gwen asked me one day, early in our relationship.

"I might," I said. "How many hours do you think it will take?"

"I don't know. Autumn's let it get away from her and it is a stinking mess."

"Will you let someone you don't know in to clean?" I asked gingerly, knowing this part of the equation would be a challenge. If the roles were reversed, I'm not sure I would let Gwen send over someone unknown to come into my home.

"Maybe," she said. "It really needs it bad, so I think it will be OK."

Offering cleaning services to frustrated clients was not something we normally did, but I thought if I could hire someone to clean Gwen's house, this would get Gwen off Autumn's back and give Autumn a bit of breathing room. I wasn't doing this for Gwen; I was doing this for Autumn.

I called one client who did housekeeping and asked her if she would take the job.

"Who is it?" she asked.

When I told her, she immediately said, "No. She's mean and her old man is crazy, and the place is filthy. I drive by it all the time. Sorry, Miss Laura. I can't do that."

I called Lorraine next. She was out of work at the time and had experience cleaning houses. After the previous call, I knew I had to tell her right up front who it was and what the situation was. "I'll do it, but I'll only do it once," she said. "I don't like those people, but I'll do it for you."

"Thank you, Lorraine. I am so grateful you'll do this. I think it will help the entire family," I said. "We'll pay you for it. Just let me know how many hours it takes and I'll write you a check. Will you call Gwen and work it out?"

A week passed before I heard back from Lorraine.

"Gwen is awful and the house was trashed, but I did what I could. I was there four hours this morning, and there are some parts of it I never got to, but I did my best," Lorraine said, her words spilling out quickly like an overflowing basin. "Don't ask me to do it again. I won't go back."

"Thank you, Lorraine. Come by anytime and get your check. I've got groceries for you, too. Thank you so much."

The house that Gwen lived in was barely a house. It was a run-down single-wide trailer stuck in the middle of a field. It had narrow concrete steps next to the front door, but there was an eight-inch gap between the steps and the door. The door opened to the outside so that if you didn't step down at least one step before entering, the door would sweep you off into the yard. With no more than six hundred square feet between the plastic walls and the cheap carpet, there was no extra space for anything, not even a door that swung to the inside.

I immediately called Gwen to get her perspective on the housecleaning project. Selfishly, I was expecting her to be grateful and appreciative. Maybe she would even apologize to me for being so hateful about the whole thing. I wanted her to understand that her anger about the house being dirty was now irrelevant and inappropriate and she could let go of all this negative energy. I didn't plan to tell her I'd never spent CAC money to have a client's house cleaned before, but I wanted her to know this was special and I expected her to have a modicum of gratitude.

As I was listening to the phone ring and waiting for her to answer, all these thoughts of self-satisfaction and expectations of thanksgiving and appreciation ran through my mind. I had—yet again—saved the day. I had solved someone else's problem and I was going to get a nice, big pat on the back for doing so. I was convinced God was smiling down, noting my goodness.

The phone kept ringing and ringing. There was no answering machine, so I let it keep ringing. Finally, someone answered it.

"Hello?" Gwen's voice was angry and gruff. She had caller ID; she knew it was me.

"Hi, Gwen, it's Laura from CAC. I just talked to Lorraine and she said your house is all cleaned up. This is great!" I was cheerful and peppy. I hoped to transmit my enthusiasm

to Gwen and hoped that by giving her positive words she might reflect them back to me. But it wasn't going to happen.

"I can't believe you sent Lorraine to clean my house. I've known her forever and she's a pill-popping good-for-nothing. She did a horrible job, and I just sent her away. I was sick of her ugly face. She didn't do anything right. She ran out of rags, and she didn't even get to the back room, and the bathroom still stinks and . . ."

Not one thing had changed.

I just listened while Gwen ranted. I wanted to argue with her and tell her the bathroom smelled like urine because her husband was drunk all the time and missed the toilet, and the kitchen was filthy because she didn't clean up after every meal, and there were fleas in the carpet because she had too many pets. But I tried to keep Autumn in the front of my mind.

"I'm sorry this didn't work out, Gwen," I said, trying to calm her down. "I know it can be frustrating to have someone else in your home. Lorraine is a good person, and she did her best. I'm glad Autumn will come home from school today and have less to do at home and more time for her homework."

Gwen didn't want any of my platitudes or smoothing over. She just wanted to complain some more. I listened for a while. I was frustrated, feeling disappointed and used. The only good things that came of this fiasco were Lorraine earned some money and could feed her family for a few days and Autumn had been helped with the cleaning work.

"Gwen, I have to go now. Someone has just walked in my office, but I'm glad we were able to help," I said, not one word of that sentence being true. No one had walked in, and I was sorry I'd ever sent anyone into her place. I had to make this conversation come to an end.

"Thanks for nothing," Gwen said, and slammed down the phone.

I hung up the phone and dropped my head into my hands—completely dejected. Gwen was so riled up that I worried she'd take out her anger next on Autumn, who would be arriving home from school on the bus in just an hour. What I thought would be a simple solution to the problem of a dirty house was self-deluded and misguided. I had only created another level of anger and hostility in a home that needed no more of either. This was yet another of those times when I completely misunderstood what was going on, on a cultural level and on an emotional level. I really didn't know what I was doing in this job.

And where was God in this? Wasn't God supposed to be helping? Would God have told me to do something different? I did the best I could, but it didn't seem to be enough.

About six weeks after the housecleaning incident, Gwen called me. This was when she told me Autumn was cutting herself.

"Do you think you could get Lorraine to come back and clean again? Autumn's out of control and she's not doing anything around the house," Gwen said. "Stupid girl is cutting herself again and it is driving me crazy." I could barely believe what I was hearing after the way our last attempt at housecleaning had turned out. I ignored that part of Gwen's request and encouraged Gwen to come in and to bring Autumn with her.

I suspected Autumn's cutting behavior was stimulated by her need to have control in one area of her life and to feel pain on her own terms. I also suspected she did it because it infuriated her mother and it was one of the only ways she had to retaliate for her mother's hateful words and actions. Maybe when she cut, she thought she controlled or limited Gwen's rages. I never knew.

About an hour after our phone call, Gwen and Autumn stood at the open door of my office. I got up and welcomed them in.

Gwen was obese, had on grimy nondescript clothes, and looked generally unhealthy. Autumn was heavy too, but she'd gotten cleaned up to come in. Her jet-black hair was highlighted with hot-pink streaks, calculatingly styled to cover half of her face. She had on a lot of makeup—teenage Goth, with thick black eyeliner and mascara and deep red lipstick emphasizing her pale skin. Underneath all this artifice and pain was a beautiful seventeen-year-old girl.

Autumn was wearing a too-tight spaghetti-strap camisole

that emphasized her large breasts, and she made no attempt to cover her scars, scabs, and wounds from cutting. She had cut her inner forearms, near her elbow on her upper arms, and—most painful of all to see—on that soft, fleshy part of the body where the arm meets the chest, that flabby piece of skin above the armpit. These were the newest cuts: red and swollen and angry.

I tried not to stare at her wounds, but my eyes were drawn to them. I wanted to touch them. I wanted to take the jar of lotion from my desk drawer and tenderly rub something on them. I wanted to take away Autumn's deep pain that led her to inflict pain on herself without shame or embarrassment.

I wanted to spit on my fingers and heal Autumn's wounds.

I wanted to soothe the angry red places I could see, and I wanted to heal her broken spirit.

I wanted to be Jesus for her.

As I looked at Autumn's wounds, I become enraged with Gwen. How could a mother let her child continue in such pain without doing one thing to try to help her? What must it be like to live in a home with so much anger and hurt? I took a deep breath and tried to remain focused on Autumn.

"Oh, honey," I said to Autumn, taking her hands in mine. She was a bit resistant to this physicality, but I kept holding on to her hands, which had bitten, black-polished nails. "It hurts me to see you hurting yourself."

Autumn just shrugged, and her eyes welled up with tears.

"She does this to herself," Gwen said. "It's her own fault.

I tell her to stop, but look how much she listens to me."
Gwen cocked her head at me then turned away.

Hearing her mother's condemnation, Autumn started crying without making any sound. Gwen was sitting across the desk from me. Autumn was sitting beside me with her back to her mother. Gwen couldn't see Autumn crying and wasn't looking at her anyway.

"You know what, Gwen," I said, squeezing Autumn's hands and watching her emotionally collapse before me, "why don't you carry some groceries out to your car and I'll visit with Autumn a minute." I stood up and handed Gwen the bag of groceries, and then walked her to the door.

Autumn was crying hard now, yet not making a sound. She seemed practiced at doing this. I wondered how many nights she'd cried herself to sleep without making a peep, chest heaving and tears streaming down her face without any noise coming out.

I knew our time was short.

"What can I do to help?" I asked.

"Get me out of that house," Autumn said, looking up at me with her eyes ablaze, mascara streaks running down her face. "Get me out of that house."

"When do you graduate?"

"This May. I can stand it until then, but I have to get out after that."

"What do you want to be when you grow up, Autumn? What are you good at? What makes you happy?"

Her face lightened up as she smiled and said, "I like make-up and hair."

"I can tell," I said. "You do a great job of it, too. Did you do your own highlights?"

"Yes," she said proudly. "I want to go to cosmetology school in Nashville so I can live there and do this all the time. I want to make other people beautiful."

"OK," I said. "This is a good plan. You need to get out of the house and go to school. Let's talk next week about a plan to make this happen."

About this time, Gwen walked in from her trip to the car. She immediately started griping at us both. "Aren't you done yet?"

I believe in not having secrets and in involving families in every way possible, so I recapped the conversation Autumn and I had just had about finishing high school and her desire to get cosmetology training. I made a pledge to both of them: "We'll do all we can to help Autumn achieve her goals of going to school, of moving to Nashville, and of making other people beautiful," I said. "We can do this, Autumn. *You* can do this. You are a beautiful person."

Upon hearing these final words, Autumn looked away uncomfortably. Gwen snorted loudly. My heart was breaking for this precious child. Did anyone ever tell her she was beautiful? Did her mother say anything positive to her? I looked at her again and saw how tender and young she was behind all the makeup and the revealing clothing and the scars from her self-mutilation. The wounds I saw so clearly were obviously not the only wounds in this girl's life.

A few weeks later, Autumn called me and asked if we could meet to talk about her plans to go to cosmetology school. She had talked to the guidance counselor at the high school and had more information. We met at my office so we could talk and then I could drive her home.

"You need to tell your mother we're doing this," I told Autumn. She said she would think about it.

Wednesday came and Autumn arrived in my office about 4 p.m. after riding the bus to Sewanee. Her makeup was toned down, although perfectly applied; her nails were a bright shade of pink; and she had on a long-sleeved, clean cotton shirt. Her highlighted hair was pushed back behind her ears so I could see all of her face. She was a lovely girl, although deeply confused and depressed.

She had done all the research and had gotten everything she needed to apply to the cosmetology school in Nashville, but it was a technical school that made no provisions for housing. She would need to find an apartment on her own. We talked through all the issues related to moving: she'd never moved before, didn't know how to go about making deposits for utilities, and had no idea what it would take to make this transition. I could tell she was getting overwhelmed. I was getting overwhelmed at the thought of this innocent girl moving to the big city all alone and not being equipped in any way for what she might encounter.

"Let's just take this one step at a time, Autumn. Rather than get swamped in the 'what ifs' of moving, let's figure out if anyone else from your school is going and see if we can't partner with them," I said. "And you need to fill out the application for the school and get it sent in. If there are any fees, we'll be happy to pay them."

"OK," Autumn said. "I'll get started on the paperwork."

It was nearing 5 p.m. and time for us both to go home. I picked up a bag full of groceries, got another bag of fresh bread, and then Autumn and I walked to my van. She asked a lot of questions about my family as we drove out to her house, many miles from downtown Sewanee. As we neared the turnoff for her house, she became very quiet.

"Autumn, are you going to be OK?"

"Yes, Miss Laura," she said.

"I don't want you to hurt yourself anymore. The plans you are making to leave are good solid plans for your future. You are beautiful and you deserve a life of happiness," I said. She looked down at her lap and said nothing.

We pulled onto the gravel driveway and headed toward the trailer. Three mangy dogs ran alongside the car as we pulled in.

"Do they bite?" I asked.

"No," Autumn said.

Autumn got her backpack and I got the bags of bread and groceries, and we walked up those concrete steps. Autumn moved back as she opened the door and walked into the trailer. It smelled of urine and cigarette smoke and sour milk and stinky shoes. I walked in behind her and saw plastic grocery bags and food wrappers and dirty ashtrays all around the living room. Two cats lounged in the squalor, curled up together in a plaid recliner with ripped fabric.

"Momma, I'm home," Autumn yelled out.

"Hi, Gwen, it's Laura. I've brought Autumn home, and I have some groceries for you."

I walked into the kitchen area, looking for any clear surface to put the bags down on. Filthy dishes covered with food rested in the sink. A cast-iron skillet half-full of hamburger and potato hash was on the stove with another cat eating from it. Empty beer cans were strewn around the counter.

"Momma, I'm home. Miss Laura's with me," Autumn shouted again.

"Come on back," a voice demanded from the narrow hallway. This was making me very nervous, very uncomfortable, very embarrassed, and a bit scared. Autumn started to lead me down the passageway to the bedrooms and bathroom. The hallway was dark. There were piles of dog feces on the carpet, near the wall.

"Autumn, I shouldn't be here. I'll just go now. Tell your mom I said hi, and call me if you need anything." I was thinking, *Please don't make me go any farther into this pitiful place where I wouldn't let my dogs live. Please, God, don't make me walk any farther in this nightmare.*

"Come on," Autumn said. "She's OK when she's like this." We walked past the bathroom, where the door was open and I could see the floor was brown with urine stains and the walls of the tub were covered in black mold.

"Autumn?" Gwen's voice barked out again. "Are you here?"

Autumn held onto my arm as we stood outside the door to the next room. Could she sense I wanted to flee, to run away as fast as I could? At the end of the hall was another closed door, and I could hear coming from that space the loud, raspy snores of a man.

"Autumn!" Gwen yelled loudly, impatiently. Autumn opened the door to the room. Gwen was sprawled on a full-size mattress, which had been laid directly on the floor. It had no sheets or coverings, just the familiar blue-and-white ticking material, and was stained with dried blood, urine, and mucus. Gwen was wearing only a bra and panties; she was lying on her side, with her eyes half open. She had no pillow, no blanket, no sheet, and no nightgown. The mattress took up almost every inch of the room. Clothes were piled on the closet floor and there was no other furniture in the space.

"Autumn!" Gwen slurred her words as she yelled, every sentence punctuated with foul language. "Where have you been? And who did you bring home with you?" Gwen was pointing at me and tried to lift her head from the mattress, but it didn't get very far. "Why are you in here anyway? Get out of here."

"It's Miss Laura, Momma. She brought me home. It's OK," Autumn said calmly. "She brought me home and she brought us some groceries."

"Laura?" bellowed Gwen. "Who's Laura and why . . ." I quickly backed away from the doorway and whispered to Autumn, "I'll wait for you up front." I backed down the hallway, still listening but moving to a place less vulnerable than watching this argument. I was scared, confused, and keenly aware I was in the middle of something and someplace I had no business in being. I was deep into another world where I was powerless.

Gwen continued to berate Autumn for another few seconds, which felt like minutes as I took in the chaos and disorder around me. Autumn tried to soothe her mother with calming words, but then she pulled the door shut and came back into the living area where I was waiting.

Autumn walked toward me and collapsed in tears in my arms.

"You are going to be OK, Autumn. You are strong, and you are beautiful, and you are smart," I said. I hugged her and held her and stroked her head and smoothed her back, the way mothers are supposed to comfort their children. She was still crying. I pulled her face out of my shoulder and looked her directly in the eyes.

"You are a blessed child of God and you are going to get

through this." I kissed my thumb and made the sign of the cross on her forehead. "God bless you and keep you safe tonight and always," I prayed to her, and for her, and with her, knowing God could hear us but wondering if God could change this place.

Autumn rested her head on my shoulder and cried some more. I just murmured all those things that every child needs to hear: "I love you. You are precious. I love you. You are beautiful. It is going to be OK. I love you."

When Autumn was finally spent from crying, she took a deep breath and said, "Thank you. I know you need to get home. Thanks for the ride."

I stepped over the trash on the floor and walked to the door. "Call me when you know more, OK?" I said as I left. Autumn nodded to me and waved good-bye.

Outside, it was pitch black and there were no floodlights to help me see my way to my car. It was one of those October nights where darkness falls faster than you imagine; we'd gone inside as the sun was setting, and now it was impossible to see anything.

The dogs barked and got tangled in my legs as I moved blindly to my van. I got inside, immediately locked the doors, and drove off as fast as I could. Once I got back to the paved road, I kept driving, but I slowed the van down and started sobbing. I was now the one with the chest heaving, unable to breathe. I couldn't believe I'd left Autumn in that terrifying place where love seemed absent and it smelled like death—

death of all kinds—emotional, physical, spiritual. And I left her. I left because I was terrified and powerless, and I didn't know what else to do.

But also I left her because I had to trust God to take care of the problems I couldn't solve, the ones that were so much bigger than a check or a bag of food could resolve. And I left her because I had a family of my own that needed me.

When I got home, it was as if nothing had happened; my family assumed I'd had just another day at the office. There was the cacophony of predinner questions: "What time are we eating?" "Where are my cleats?" "Can I watch TV?" "Do we have any graph paper?" Yet I moved through my clean, comfortable house with numbness and shock at what I'd just seen. I wanted to yell at my own children, "Do you know how lucky you are? You could have been born into a different family and this would all be a dream!" But I knew it wasn't their fault that Autumn had been born into such a complicated, broken family.

When I arrived at the office the next day, Gwen had left a rambling message on the answering machine. The gist of it was that Autumn, "that liar," had told Gwen that Gwen had "cussed Laura out" and Gwen said she would "never do something like that because Laura is a good Christian woman who has helped us a lot."

I didn't call her back—there was no need in pointing out that Autumn was right and Gwen was wrong. It was a reminder to me of how far from reality Gwen was living, either because of illness or addiction, and how sick she really was.

Just a few weeks after taking Autumn home that night, I read in the county paper that Gwen and her husband had sold their land in Sewanee. They must have moved away. I never heard from Autumn again about going to cosmetology school. I don't know if she suffered retribution at the hands of Gwen or the snoring, scary father. After that, Gwen would call me from time to time from another city, wanting help with her light bill. I told her no each time and reminded her that we couldn't help her since she had moved away. I always asked about Autumn.

"Where's she at? What's she doing?" I inquired in my peppy, positive voice.

"Don't know and don't care," Gwen answered the last time we spoke.

Good for Autumn, is all I could think. *Good for you, strong, smart, beautiful girl. Stay as far away from that toxic chaos as possible.* Autumn knew CAC was there for her whenever she needed it. Thank God she took her chance and got out. Though I was powerless to change Autumn's family, I was not powerless when it came to offering Autumn God's generous love. Through me, God showed Autumn how special and precious she was during those weeks we had together. I still hold on to those times of grace. I hope Autumn does too.

Chapter
ELEVEN

CONFESSION

and

CALLING

To be a Christian means to forgive the inexcusable because God has forgiven the inexcusable in you.

—C. S. LEWIS

WHETHER I WAS LISTENING TO A YOUNG girl's dreams of her future or to a dying mother's wishes for her children, I heard many confessions while sitting at the desk at CAC. It wasn't quite like the Catholic confessionals in the movies, with doors and privacy screens, but something sacred about that space caused people to come in and tell me their secrets. It didn't matter that they were sitting on folding chairs among stacks of canned goods and cases of dried beans.

I don't know why they did it. I didn't ever ask, "Are you sure you want to tell me this?" I just listened quietly, nodding when I needed to, asking questions only when there was a lot of space left for me to probe. I offered tissues when tears came. I prayed aloud when asked. I prayed silently through each of those powerful and intimate conversations. I prayed to God to please heal our friend. Please give him or her strength to do the right thing. Please forgive him or her.

The prayer book has directions for the priest after a confession: "Here the priest may offer counsel, direction, and comfort." Though I was without the stole or the collar of a priest, I tried to do the same. Usually I had no counsel or direction to offer, though. Only comfort.

I had my own petitions to God during these sessions, *Please God, let me not look shocked or disbelieving. Please restrain my hands even though I want to write this down because I won't believe it when it is over. Please let me be a compassionate listener, not a judging presence right now.*

I listened. I listened deeply. I listened quietly. I just listened.

I listened to the voices of broken families, of lost children, of wounded spouses. I listened to the sounds of sadness and loss, of shame and embarrassment, of confusion and mystery. And I heard each one of these people searching for something more in his or her life—something better.

"I know everyone in this town who smokes marijuana, because I grow the best weed around," Matt told me. "We've got this hydroponic greenhouse and we hand-pollinate the weed ourselves." Then, bragging, he said, "If you want me to, I can tell you which adults still smoke weed, which high school kids smoke, and who buys which kind."

I asked him how he got into this, since he barely finished high school.

"Oh, my dad taught it all to me. We've been doing it for years."

I tried not to look shocked or appalled. This was how Matt felt he was part of our community.

"My momma taught me how to cook meth," Tiffany said, using the shorthand term for methamphetamines, the highly addictive drug that has become a serious problem in rural America. "Momma needed help one day, so she showed me how."

By the time I met them, Tiffany, her mother, and her sister were all using meth. Then Tiffany slashed at her boyfriend's neck with a butcher knife while he was driving their van on the Fourth of July. It was only a flesh wound, but it got her thrown in jail for attempted murder and made him "right angry," Tiffany's sister said. Tiffany came by CAC when she got out on bail. She was using meth again—her eyes were runny and dilated as she stumbled toward me with one of her sloppy wet kisses. "I love you, Miss Laura, I love you so much," she said, as she always did.

I don't doubt that Tiffany really loved me, but I never knew what condition she was in when she said it. If she had been drug-free, would she have felt the same way? Would she even have come to see me?

"I want to kill my husband. Me and Jimmy talk about it all the time. We think about poisoning his food or shooting him or smothering him in the night. Is that awful?" Pearl asked me one day when she had hoisted her three-hundred-plus-pound body out of her car to meet me at the parish hall door. Her knees were so ruined by her obesity that she couldn't climb the four stairs to my office.

"I know your husband has treated you and your son very badly, Pearl," I said. "I can understand why you would feel that way. He's abusive and vengeful and makes your life a living hell. No one can blame you for feeling that way."

"But we really want to kill him," she said.

"I know," I said. "But, you know that you can't. You would end up in jail and your life would be no better. Please don't kill him. Why don't you call the police when he starts in on you?"

"Oh, no," Pearl said, as if I'd suggested something ghastly. "He says if we call the law he'll kill us when he gets out. And he would, too."

Pearl's husband was a diabetic and an alcoholic, so they hoped he would fall into a coma and die on his own.

What must their home look like? What must it be like to

live with such conflict? They simply wanted peace, and they were willing to kill for it.

Pearl struggled to make it to the office for groceries, but she wouldn't let me deliver groceries to her. In a way, I was glad she wouldn't let me visit. I didn't want to see another home like Autumn and Gwen's.

And then the words from friends, subtle confessions mingled with my own questions about calling: "You're already a priest; you know that Laura," an older man said to me at the office one day. "You've been ordained by this community as someone who helps people get closer to God. The church may not ordain you, but this place already has."

I didn't know how to respond, so I said nothing.

Then he quickly moved our conversation to a mutual acquaintance whom we both distrusted. He said, "You're wearing your stole now, right?" he asked.

I nodded my assent.

"I think she's stealing money from a lot of people."

I nodded again.

"I've never been able to tell anyone this before."

I nodded a final time. I said nothing.

"I want what you have," said a friend over breakfast one morning at the Waffle House. I told her I didn't understand what she was talking about.

"I want what you have. I want to be filled with God and the Spirit the way you are. Can you help me?"

"But I'm just as broken and confused as everyone else," I told my friend. "There's nothing I have that you don't have or have access to."

"No, you've got something I want," she said.

Another friend made a snarky comment in a meeting, not knowing she had deeply offended one of the people around the table. My friend was very upset when she learned what she had done; she felt embarrassed and contrite.

"I need you to be my priest, Laura. Can I talk to you about what just happened?"

"Of course," I said. And I listened.

At times it felt like I had no option but to be ordained. People treated me as a priest, called me a priest, and spoke to me as a priest. I was practically a priest—but not quite.

And so I lived in the tension between the laity and the ordained, between those who celebrate the sacraments in a public, official setting and those who celebrate them in the small, tender ways of everyday life. I tried to draw these two worlds nearer to each other so that what felt like a vast chasm might close.

I knew that being a priest was no different from living any life committed to Christ. It was no more important a calling than being a generous friend or a loving sister. Being a priest is acting with love and compassion, day in and day out, toward people you know and care for, as well as toward the strangers who frighten you. Any of us can do it. But serving the Eucharist to both friends and strangers at the altar of a church—this longing remained in me.

A wise friend said to me, regarding in my wrestling about the priesthood: "You must decide if this is the death you have to die." He was right. Becoming a priest is a death. Being a Christian is a death, too—death to your old self; death to ego; death to the world's priorities. Following any call of God means dying to something else.

Richard Rohr, a Franciscan friar and director of another CAC, the Center for Action and Contemplation, describes it this way

> Real holiness doesn't feel like holiness; it just feels like you're dying. It feels like you're losing it. And you are! You are losing the false self. . . . You know that God is doing this in you and with you when you can somehow smile, and trust that what you lost is something you did not need anyway.[1]

Losing your false self means losing who you thought you were. It means believing that God is working in you to make you better—to make you wholly you, wholly like Christ.

When I find myself clinging to my craving for affection and esteem, power and control, and security and survival, I know I am not on the path God wants for me.[2] Through the words of others, through contemplative prayer, and through silence, I can be quiet and still. I can let die the life that I thought I could control; let die my ego as well as my shame over letting it rule me. This, then and now, is my final calling no matter what shape my vocation takes.

No friends or clients checked to see if I was wearing a priest's collar when they shared with me their personal passions and private disclosures. We didn't enter a special space for these conversations. We sat in a small room turned food pantry, on cold metal chairs, finding our way to truth.

By listening to these confessions I recognized my own need to confess. Like Matt, I wanted to belong. Like Pearl, I wanted to survive. Like Tiffany, I tried to fill my emptiness with something that would never satisfy. And my own confession needed to be part of my vocation. It needed to be more important than any job title. Because living into our calling means knowing who we are before God.

The traditional confession service in the *Book of Common Prayer* begins with the solemn sentence: "Bless me, for I have sinned." I like the more contemporary version that directs the penitent to say, "Pray for me, a sinner."

In the daily and the extraordinary, and through all the questions, I say these words: "Pray for me, a sinner."

Chapter
TWELVE

MIRIAM'S
Second
DEATH

We have been called to heal wounds,
to unite what has fallen apart,
and to bring home those who have lost their way.
—SAINT FRANCIS OF ASSISI

M IRIAM REALLY DIED THIS TIME—DIED AND couldn't be resuscitated; died and wasn't coming back; died and broke her mother's heart.

When Miriam was alive, albeit connected to tubes and machines and monitors, I faced the dilemma of baptizing her mother, Rebecca. With Miriam's death, I faced a dilemma again. God had opened up a clear space for me to baptize Rebecca. Would I now be called on to bury her child?

Sometimes we discover our vocation by finding what doesn't bring us peace, what doesn't give life to ourselves or others.

★

About a week before Miriam's death, Rebecca called and told me that Miriam was back in the hospital in Chattanooga, where she'd been so many times before.

"Can we get some gas money for the trips?" she asked between sobs of grief. There seemed to be nothing left of Rebecca when she was done talking, just the sound of her gasping for air. I told her I would take the money right down to the gas station so they could go whenever they needed.

A few days later, Carter Gilkerson came in for his weekly visit.

"Did you hear?" he said. "That Morgan baby died down in Chattanooga last night. They've sure had a time of it with that little one. So sad."

I paused before I could say anything. I had known this would be the likely outcome given all that had happened before: Miriam's premature birth, her months in the neonatal ICU, coming home with feeding tubes and breathing monitors, and the extraordinary care it took to keep her alive. Then I had my private fears: that Miriam's "first death" had left her greatly impaired and that her parents would struggle with the basics of caring for such a severely disabled child. I snapped out of my worries to respond to Carter.

"Yes, Carter, it is really sad." I then asked him when the services would be and if Jason and Rebecca had already returned.

"No," he said. "The baby just died last night. Frances heard about it from LouAnn." Like so many of my clients, they all seem to be friends and relatives of one another. Their family trees were not independent oaks but more like gnarled wisteria.

"We'll let you know when we hear. Thanks for the bread." He picked up a few loaves of day-old sandwich bread, gave me a long, strong hug, and walked out.

After Carter left, I sat at my desk, stilled by the news. I could only guess how I would handle a similar situation. I have two children. What would I do if one of them died? I would be hysterical with grief and anger. I would be curled up in a ball, unable to function. I would want to die, too.

I moved through the rest of my morning doing the things I normally do at work. I paid electric bills for a few clients and listened to voice messages from people needing groceries. I visited with our church secretary and told her of Miriam's death—wanting to talk about it with somebody. I updated computer files and ordered food online from Second Harvest Food Bank. But, really, what I was doing was waiting—waiting for the phone call from Rebecca; waiting to hear about Miriam's death from her; waiting to see what they needed on this tragic day: a priest? a counselor? a friend?

After lunchtime, Rebecca staggered through the door. She was propped up by her mother, both of them moving through a fog of pain. Rebecca's eyes were tiny slits in her puffy and blotchy face; her hair was wild and unbrushed. Her mother looked tired and pitiful, her face smeared with mascara, one shoulder weighed down with a tote bag stuffed with papers and folders.

Rebecca started sobbing, her body shaking all over.

"She died. Miriam died. She's gone. My baby's gone."

Her voice was strong and she had neither shame nor peace in her. She wailed and moaned as she fell into my arms, and I rocked her as if she were a small child. I was still standing, but Rebecca was collapsed into my body. Every inch of her trembled as I stroked her head and murmured to her, "I know, I know . . . I'm so sorry . . . " With her mother standing behind her, Rebecca was sandwiched between two older women who loved her, but neither of us could take from her the pain she was experiencing. We could only hold her up when she couldn't stand alone.

Rebecca stopped crying and asked for a tissue. She sat down in one of the folding chairs. Her eyes were swollen and red, but I noticed her pupils were dilated wide open. Someone—maybe a doctor, maybe a friend—had given her a drug to help her get through this. I caught myself judging her and then quickly reminded myself that if I'd just lost a child, I'd want some Valium or a tumbler full of bourbon or both.

While I was considering how poorly I would be handling this cruel loss, Rebecca spoke up, asking me to do the impossible. "We want you to do Miriam's funeral," Rebecca said. "Since you baptized me, I want you to bury Miriam."

I didn't know what to say. I couldn't even consider doing this funeral. I wouldn't do it because I knew that in some small-town weekly newspaper an obituary would read, "Miriam Shakira Morgan, infant daughter of Rebecca and Jason Morgan, died . . . Funeral arrangements were handled by Jones Funeral Home with Laura L. Willis presiding." It was one thing for me to baptize Rebecca in a moment when she was close to Jesus and wanted a ritual to affirm her commitment on a rainy day in a quiet church. It was another thing to help her bury her child.

"Rebecca, I'm honored, but I cannot do Miriam's funeral. There are rules, and not just rules of the church, but rules of the funeral home and beyond that keep me from doing it," I said. I didn't know if a word of this was true, but I had to find a way out of the situation. I did not want to be—should not be—the person who buried Miriam.

This, I discovered, was the danger of playing priest. I had gotten away with it for years, being priestlike when it was easy or expedient or downright fun. I could be someone else when I wanted to, and leave it behind when I felt like it. The problem with this fantasy I'd been acting out was that sometimes other people started believing you, and the next thing you knew, they wanted you to do something real, something hard, something that required more than you had to give. Sitting with Rebecca, I found myself glad I wasn't ordained. I simply said no. I knew it was the coward's path, but I also knew the answer should be no.

Rebecca started crying again. "We don't know anyone else, and we want you to do it," she said. "Please."

"I'll find a priest for you," I said. "That's how I can help."

"But, we really, really want you," she pleaded.

Rebecca was quietly weeping again, but then she laid her head down. Exhaustion, desperation, medication—now she was falling asleep right on my old wooden desk. She was spent.

"The visitation is tonight, from six to eight, at the funeral home," her mother said. "The funeral is tomorrow at two. I hope you can find someone to do the service. We'd really hoped you would do it."

"I'll find someone," I promised.

She said thank you and scooped up her broken daughter, virtually carrying her out of my office.

I still had not found a priest when I went to the funeral home for the visitation that evening. Before going into the chapel, I went first to the funeral home office to see if the family had found someone. Jason's cousin told me Sister Lucy from St. Mary's Convent had agreed to do it.

"That's good news," I said, deeply relieved.

"Is Miriam going to be buried in O'Dear?" I asked, trying to figure out which cemetery we would be going to tomorrow.

"No, they're going to have her cremated," Jason's cousin said. "They don't know what to do with her ashes yet. They're still in too much shock."

I left the office and shut the door. Why do I think I have to solve every person's problem? I hated my conceit and my pride and my raging ego. But I had to move past my self-loathing and go see Rebecca.

As I prepared to attend the visitation, I was reminded again of how foreign many parts of my clients' lives were to me, whether it was their funeral traditions or their child-hoods or their educational background. It was as if we lived in two spheres, right next to each other, that had little over-lap for me except when I sat in my office, surrounded by bags of groceries.

As I walked down the green-carpeted passageway toward the chapel that evening, I braced myself for what I expected to encounter next: the sad music, the grieving Rebecca, her family's friends who would be strangers to me, and most of all, the child we all loved who was gone. It was getting dark outside and the lights of the parking lot cast an odd amber glow through the picture windows that revealed only asphalt and old cars. The twilight mixed with the streetlights sent my internal gyroscope spinning. It was surreal. Timeless.

Moving through the doorway into the chapel jolted me from my quiet, dark void. A lot of people sat in pews in the back, with a few folks scattered closer up. Rebecca and Jason were in the front row on the right side, and a few more peo-ple were talking quietly with them.

But it was the dead child on the altar that shocked me most of all. Little Miriam, not even a year old, made to look peaceful and asleep, was strapped into her car seat. Small stuffed animals encircled the tiny lifeless body and the seat's handle was up, as if her parents would soon carry her home. Her face was serene, her eyes closed, her clothes pristine, and her legs neatly covered with a white fleece baby blanket.

Before I could make sense of this confusing tableau, everything changed again. I heard a deep moaning sound and I looked up to see Rebecca drop from her pew to the floor and crawl on her hands and knees to the low table where Miriam was placed. Rebecca draped herself half on the table and half on the floor, wailing before Miriam's body. Jason stayed in the pew, hunched over with his head in his hands, his shoulders shaking with silent sobs. Rebecca's mother moved to the floor and stroked Rebecca's head, saying, "It's OK, baby. It's OK, honey. It's OK."

Rebecca was keening as she had in my office, "She's gone. My baby's gone. I want my baby back. She's dead. My baby's dead. I want her back. I want my baby."

As Rebecca moved to Miriam's body, I sat down next to Frances Gilkerson. Carter hadn't come inside. He'd driven Frances to the funeral home, but he wouldn't come in with her.

"This is awful," I whispered to Frances.

"I've never seen nothing like this," Frances said softly. Frances had decades more experience attending funerals than I did. Maybe if Miriam had been in a casket it would have been easier. Maybe if she'd been cremated already, it wouldn't have been so painful. But Miriam waited in her car seat, all ready to go for a ride.

Rebecca's mother finally picked her daughter up and moved her back to the pew, where she continued to sob.

While Frances sat with dignity and serenity, my mind was racing. How can I make this situation better? But I realized no person—pastor or priest, parent or prophet—could cure what was ailing Rebecca. The only thing I could do was be a witness: to friendship and compassion, to pain and grieving. *Please help, God,* I prayed. *Let me know what to do. Please. God. Help.*

I got up, kissed Frances good-bye on the cheek, and walked up the aisle to the front of the chapel.

I knelt in front of Rebecca and hugged her. She started sobbing loudly again. I told her how sorry I was that Miriam had died. I told her that Miriam was with God and that God would comfort her. Rebecca looked up at me with those deadened, empty eyes, and I realized she didn't understand a word I'd said. She was deeply drugged. Rebecca's mother leaned over to me and said, "Rebecca's not doing very well. I know she appreciates all you've done for them."

I left the visitation confused, shocked, and despondent.

The next day, I did what I knew to do. I arrived at the funeral home early and asked in the office if Jason and Rebecca needed help paying for the funeral expenses. The family had taken up a collection to cover the costs, Jason's cousin told me. It wasn't too much since there was no casket, she said.

When I walked into the chapel for the funeral service, Miriam's body sat in her car seat again, on the altar, waiting for the funeral to begin. She was still wrapped in her white baby blanket, still surrounded by the stuffed animals, still fully dressed, and still looking as if she were asleep. The only difference was now the handle of the car seat was pulled back so that Miriam's body was propped up and everyone could see her.

Traditional funeral hymns played quietly through the sound system, hymns I knew by heart from my days in the Baptist Church: "Softly and Tenderly Jesus Is Calling," "I Come to the Garden Alone," and "Just as I Am." Rebecca and Jason sat in the same place as the night before, as if they'd never left the building. Sister Lucy, wearing her clerical collar and black cassock, was seated in the other front pew, across the aisle from Rebecca and Jason. She sat alone, quietly, waiting to begin the service.

The pews held no prayer books or hymnals or Bibles. Sister Lucy used the Episcopal funeral liturgy. Only a few of us in the assembled gathering knew what to say, but then there aren't many responses for the congregation in the funeral service. Most of the people weren't Episcopalians anyway, and they simply stood and sat when Sister Lucy gestured to them. She began the service with her resonant voice:

I am Resurrection and I am Life, says the Lord.
Whoever has faith in me shall have life,
even though he die.
And everyone who has life,
and has committed himself to me in faith,
shall not die for ever.

As for me, I know that my Redeemer lives
and that at the last he will stand upon the earth.
After my awaking, he will raise me up;
and in my body I shall see God.
I myself shall see, and my eyes behold him
who is my friend and not a stranger.[1]

Those opening words of the funeral liturgy—the anthem—are a stark reminder of all that is important to God, and important in life, in just a few perfect lines. We are the Lord's possession, no matter if we live or if we die. Sister Lucy read with great solemnity and reverence as the group collectively wept.

Sister Lucy gave a short homily about the shock of the sudden death of a child and how it feels as if God is absent from such an act. She encouraged Jason and Rebecca and all of us to have faith in God, no matter how great our grief.

Sister Lucy—a faithful pastor who had helped families like this one through all forms of death and loss and pain—never once looked down at the table where Miriam rested. She never seemed disturbed at the way Miriam's parents had prepared her for this service. She never did anything that drew attention to herself or even to Miriam. She focused on God through it all, and in doing so, helped everyone keep their focus on God, too.

I could not have performed that service. Witnessing it, I understood why it was so important to tell Rebecca no. I would have been anxious wondering why Miriam was on that altar table without a coffin and why we were pretending she was simply asleep. I would have been distracted by Rebecca's heart-wrenching cries and Jason's soft moans. I would have felt out of place leading this family through another Episcopal service that they didn't know and that I was not ordained to do or prepared to provide.

But Sister Lucy moved through Miriam's funeral with God's grace and peace. Sister Lucy was fulfilling her calling.

And I learned, too, that I was fulfilling mine. I listened as Carter told me of Miriam's death. I sat with Frances and shared this curious funeral. I offered Rebecca and her family a loving presence during those days and beyond. I followed where God's peace was, trusting that God would use my calling to bring peace to others, too.

Chapter

THIRTEEN

VISIONS

of

JOY

*Joy is a mystery because it can happen anywhere, anytime,
even under the most umpromising circumstances, even in
the midst of suffering, with tears in its eyes.*
—FREDERICK BUECHNER

WHEN I FIRST BEGAN MY WORK AT CAC AND people offered me gifts—jars of jam and pickles, handmade crafts, a bouquet of wildflowers in a mayonnaise jar—I would accept them, say thank you, and then turn around and give them to someone else. I had a hard time truly accepting anything, especially from people who I knew were in need.

Over the years I learned that receiving a gift means humbling myself, acknowledging that I really do need what someone else can offer. It means recognizing my own poverty. And I learned that, like God, gifts often show up when they are least expected.

Our ministry at CAC was a movement of gifts, in and out, every week. People across the community hosted food drives or toiletry drives and brought the items in. Scouts arrived with boxes and crates of food they had collected by walking around town, leaving grocery bags on doorsteps, and going back a week later to gather the filled bags. College students brought bags of extra shampoo and conditioner they'd bought on trips to the store. People moving out at the end of the semester (college students, seminarians, adjunct faculty) emptied their pantries and shelves to our office. Sometimes the items were in pristine condition. Other times there would be half-eaten boxes of cereal (to the trash), almost-full bottles of detergent (saved and given away), cases of ramen noodles (happily redistributed), or single-serving pouches of macaroni and cheese or instant oatmeal and cocoa (dropped in this week's grocery bags).

On Pantry Sunday, the first Sunday of the month at area churches, people wanted to participate even if they had forgotten to buy food during the week, so they would cull their own shelves for items they no longer needed or could easily replace. The Pantry Sunday offerings were often a funny collection of the boring (chicken noodle soup, tuna fish, kidney beans) and the bizarre (she-crab soup, marinated artichoke hearts, sliced jalapeños, and Twining's tea). The most unusual item ever donated to CAC was a jar of vermouth-soaked cocktail onions, something one might use when making martinis—not a regular beverage of the Appalachian poor.

Whenever these stranger items came into the office, we set them on a special shelf. Volunteers and board members and parishioners might come in and say, "I love . . . ," and I would encourage them to take that item—garlic-stuffed olives, for example—and bring back a jar of peanut butter. It was an even exchange: they got something they wanted and we got something we could use. The Indian curry mixes, water chestnuts, and anchovies all got moved through like this.

On occasion, a mother would call to tell me her child had been collecting money for the hungry. I always encouraged her to let the child deliver the money so I could thank her or him in person. I received dozens of Ziploc bags full of coins—nickels and pennies and quarters, all poured in together—from generous children in our community. I could see that these young children were truly concerned for the needs of others.

Children were also a special, essential part of the volunteer pool. Just as the ones at the elementary school carried no preset anxieties about the work, neither did the preschoolers. Looking back at the daily logs of activity over those ten years, I found that children who are now in middle and high school had years ago printed their names so carefully that they took two lines of the paper, with their primitive hand-writing. All the children who helped wanted their name to be in that book, to record their work, to let someone know they cared, no matter what their age.

Virtually every client said thank you to me sometime, somehow. Sometimes clients got angry with me because I didn't give them exactly what they wanted. Sometimes they took out their frustrations on me, much as a child throws a tantrum at home with those whom they most love. Sometimes the gratitude took shape as words and hugs. Sometimes it was a card or note.

One client, Audrey, didn't read or write or drive. We helped pay for her husband's funeral expenses and paid her water and electric bills the month he died. I didn't see her for many months after that because she lived in a remote cove and had no way to get to the office. I wondered how she was doing, but I figured her children were taking care of her. And they were.

One day, Audrey appeared for a breakfast. It was a chilly Wednesday morning. Audrey arrived with her sister; her son had driven them. Audrey carried in her arms a large yellow plastic bag—the largest size the Dollar Store had—and handed it to me.

"What's this?" I asked, genuinely delighted.

"I made it for you, Miss Laura," Audrey said. "I wanted to do something to thank you for all you did for us."

"Should I open it here or do you want to go someplace private?"

By now, a small crowd had gathered around me in the office, and Audrey was beaming with pride.

"Go on, open it," she said.

Inside the bag was a beautifully hand-stitched, hand-pieced king-size quilt, in a nine-patch pattern. It was made from scraps—not handpicked fabrics from an expensive crafting store, but leftover scraps from clothing Audrey had made for her children and grandchildren, pieces of her husband's shirts, and simple navy blue and white patterned cotton cloth that linked all the squares together. The backing was a soft, faded sheet with yellow roses on it. Pulling it close to me, I felt as if I were wrapping myself in Audrey's life.

"Oh, Audrey," I cried. "It is beautiful. You made this? It is incredible. Are you sure I should keep it?"

"I wanted you to have something from us," Audrey said.

It was the first of three quilts Audrey made for me while I was at CAC. At my house, we keep them in our den on the couch. We fight over who gets to use them. They are warm and infused with love. They are a piece of Audrey and her family.

Each time Audrey gave me a quilt, she wanted everyone around to see it. She was proud of her handiwork, and with good reason. Each time, I sent her a handwritten thank-you letter that I mailed to her house. Someone she knew read her mail to her, I knew. I wanted her to know how much the quilts meant to me and that I never took her gifts for granted.

Over the years, I got to accept all kinds of beautiful, precious gifts. An older woman made me a Fourth of July wreath of yarn and miniature American flags. Numerous people brought me jars of apple butter and strawberry jam when they finished their canning for the season. One man brought me the teaching certificate he earned with CAC's help. One woman brought me her grades each semester to show me her progress at college.

Gifts, all of these. Gifts to God, really, offered to me because of this work, just as gifts carried to the altar in church are handed to a minister. The gifts I received may have been quilts and cards and photographs, but they were no less precious than the gifts of the Magi at the birth of Christ. They came from God, just as the food we offered came from God. All of them, in turn, returned as thanks to God.

Over the years, I saw my own need. I saw God in the hands reached out to me. And I received.

Chapter
FOURTEEN

THE HANDS

of

JESUS

What does love look like? It has the hands to help others.

It has the feet to hasten to the poor and needy.

It has eyes to see misery and want.

It has the ears to hear the sighs and sorrows of men.

—SAINT AUGUSTINE OF HIPPO

I SPENT A LOT OF TIME WORKING WITH MY hands during my ten years at CAC: unpacking cardboard cases of food, repacking food into grocery bags, serving breakfast to clients and schoolchildren, and holding the hands of others. My nails were always short, my cuticles ragged. It took many hands to make the ministry possible—hands to give and hands to receive.

During those years, and since then, I was often the chalice bearer at my beloved parish, offering the cup of wine at the smooth oak Communion rail on Sunday mornings, saying the words that I loved, the same words I said to Rebecca and her mother: "The blood of Christ, the cup of salvation."

There I learned that in a close-knit community it is possible to recognize people by their hands alone. At Communion, I could identify every person without looking at his or her face as that person came to rest his or her hands on that rail. Each person's hands were known to me, known to one another, and most important, known to God. I knew the pattern of how each pair of hands folded together—whose hands were wrinkled and gnarled; who had the hands of laborers and who had the hands of professors; who had young, smooth hands; and whose hands shook with disease. Without hearing a word from these friends or ever looking up, I knew them.

Those moments watching the hands of my community pass in front of me remind me of how intimately God knows us. God knows the oddities and beauties of our hands, the way they show our work and prayers and joys. And of course God's understanding of us goes far beyond our skin, our fingers, our understanding of one another. It is God who knows us when we don't even know ourselves.

When I got to Frances and Carter's home on a summer Saturday morning, Frances's hands looked worse than ever. For almost two weeks, her palms had been angry, red, swollen, peeling, and scabby. Despite this, she had continued to cook every meal, wash every dish, and do every load of laundry. That day a group had gathered, not for help with weekend chores, but to witness Frances and Carter sign their wills: legal documents to secure the future of the Gilkerson family, protect Frances amd Carter as they aged, and prepare them as they moved toward death. This was housekeeping, but of a vastly more serious sort.

Frances and Carter and the attorney sat at the kitchen table. My friend Kay and I stood nearby. Witt, the lawyer, passed out pens and talked with Frances and Carter about the papers, ensuring they knew what they were doing. Each page had to be initialed or signed. Sometimes, Frances looked at me, confused, and I leaned over, whispered to her about what was on the page, and pointed to the place where she needed to sign. But her hands hurt so much that she could barely hold the pen. She kept putting it down to rub her sore hands together.

At some point during the signing, I sat down on the linoleum floor next to Frances so it would be easier to answer her questions. Near the end of the last document, her will, a quiet hush fell over the group. Signing one's will is a stark reminder that each of us will die. I touched Frances's hands and quietly asked her if she wanted me to pray over her before I left. She nodded.

When the paperwork was finished, Carter and Kay and Witt were standing near the front door talking while Frances and I stayed at the kitchen table. I got on my knees in front of her; held her swollen, red hands in my hands; and I prayed. I prayed for healing and comfort and release from the pain she was experiencing. I prayed for her long, success-ful marriage and the steps she and Carter had just taken to ensure their family's future. I prayed for their vast family. And I came back to her hands.

"Bless these hands, dear God." And as I prayed, I kissed each peeling palm and then placed them on my cheeks. I held them to my face as you might cradle a child's face with your own hands. "Comfort Frances and shine your healing light on her during this time of pain."

Perhaps there was talking going on around us. Perhaps everyone in the room was watching Frances and me. I don't know. Something greater than me was at work, something that told me how to pray with Frances.

I wanted to be Jesus for her, to touch her wounded places and make them whole.

And Frances did the same for me. She became Jesus for me in those moments. Her hands touched my face and healed my pain and made me whole, in the way that only Jesus can do.

I have no illusions that anything I did cured Frances's hands. That wasn't the point. It was an impromptu prayer on a busy Saturday morning that drew us closer to each other and closer to God that day.

A physician later told Frances that the pain came from a chemical burn from the pesticides on some squash she had prepared. Her hands began to get better. Steroids helped.

Now Frances's hands are just fine. I hold them when I go visit her and Carter, just as I would hold the hands of any of my older friends that I visit. But praying with her hands on my face, and kissing those broken and raw palms, changed me. It gave me the chance to know how it feels—for just a few moments—to be Jesus for someone else, to be Christ on this earth.

It also gave me the chance to receive Jesus, to feel His broken hands on my face and let Him heal my wounds. It was a reminder that as I offered God to others, God was offering Himself to me.

So while I was searching for an answer to my vocational questions, I realized my work was right in front of me: to be Christ for others and to let them be Christ for me; to understand that following God's calling begins with recognizing my own need for nourishment, for healing, and for help—my own hunger for food from the hands of Christ.

Epilogue

FINDING
God

No *pessimist ever discovered the secret of the stars,*
or sailed to an uncharted land, or opened a
new doorway for the human spirit.
—HELEN KELLER

IN THE SUMMER OF 2010, CAC HOSTED A MOBILE
food pantry—a one-day event that brought in more than
twenty thousand pounds of food to give to anyone who
needed help. Hosting these pantries was akin to setting up a
grocery store at dawn, distributing its entire inventory in an
orderly and fair manner throughout the day, and breaking it
down before dark. It was one of the biggest annual events of
CAC, feeding people from all across the region.

Kay, who witnessed the signing of Frances and Carter's
wills with me, handled the logistics of the food. I handled the
volunteers, the visitors at the pantry, and the publicity.

We had hosted a similar event in 2009, so we knew what

to expect. A tractor trailer from the regional food bank arrived at 7:30 a.m. We off-loaded the food, sorted it, counted it, and arranged it by 10 a.m. in the enormous building the college lent us for free.

I assigned volunteers to each station to give away the food and partnered each guest with a volunteer, the guest's "personal shopper," who helped her or him through the makeshift store. When each guest was done shopping, a volunteer carried the groceries to the guest's vehicle. One longtime client told me afterward, "I felt like a queen. I'd never been treated so nice at the grocery. No one's ever taken my food out to my car for me."

People came from our community and also from places far beyond. Some folks drove fifty miles for one cart of groceries. Everyone knew beforehand to bring a couple of cardboard boxes and a cooler (we had fresh vegetables, milk, and meat), but moving those items as they waited in line was difficult. So people put them on the ground, sitting on them when the line stopped and scooting them on the sidewalk when the line moved. The scraping sound of cardboard and plastic being shoved across pavement was ubiquitous.

The first year we did the pantry, the line of people waiting snaked around three buildings on campus. For hours, people waited in the hot August sun for a cartload of free groceries. But they waited patiently. We ran out of water early in the day, so we sent volunteers to every store in the area to buy up all the bottled water. In the second year, we were prepared and had lemonade, hot dogs, and chips for folks who waited through lunch. On that day, everyone was fed, in that moment and for many days after.

The lines of people outside, combined with the rows of people inside, along with those who had come to help—it was not so different from Sundays at my church as the Eucharist begins. Hungry souls patiently stand in line, with a sense of need, moving toward the abundance that awaits them. Others stand behind the rail preparing the feast. The ushers, like our grocery carriers and parking lot volunteers, keep the lines moving in the right direction. During the mobile pantry, nourishment came in boxes and coolers. At church, it comes from a taste of wine and a bite of bread. All are gifts of God to feed our empty places.

The final pantry ran smoothly. More than two hundred volunteers helped distribute food to more than four hundred fifty families. Through this little local ministry tucked away in the old parish hall of a church, hundreds of people had an opportunity to see God—to see God as they gave away juice boxes and crackers, cans of soup and fruit, jars of jelly and tubs of peanut butter; to see God as their cars filled with more groceries than most had ever seen; to see God in the eyes of the stranger; to see God in the hands of the giver. Just as my journey of feeding the hungry day after day was a way for God to feed me, community events like these opened up space for God to feed all of us.

I knew that this mobile food pantry would be my last as director of CAC. The editor and publisher of our weekly, free community newspaper had called me earlier that summer, setting something big in motion with a short question: "I'm going to retire. Do you want the paper?"

I answered yes without hesitation. I didn't understand what I was agreeing to, but I knew it was the next step God was asking me to take on this journey.

It was simpler than I thought it would be. I didn't see it coming. I didn't make a long-range plan for it or set it as a goal and mark my progress toward it. It just appeared. It interrupted.

I had learned to love better and more deeply in my work at the CAC. I had learned to see God in the faces of my clients, in the strangers who came by, and in the young people who helped out. Maybe that is why I knew I couldn't stay. I had learned what I needed to. God had shown me my hunger, my emptiness, each day. And God had fed me, too.

This ministry, so needed in our community, was about a living, breathing God, accessible to anyone. All that "free love" still needed to spread around, but it needed someone with fresh ideas to spread it. It was time for someone else to sit behind that desk and hear the chronicles of pain and sadness, to celebrate the new babies born, host breakfasts with schoolchildren, pack groceries with college students, listen to the confessions, and go to the funerals. It took ten years for me to get comfortable in that role, but I was there—and I could let someone else experience the joy of feeding the hungry and caring for the poor.

★

Now I publish the little newspaper in our village. We affectionately call it the "Good News Newspaper," not because of any gospel passages we put in it, but because we are careful to convey news that builds up our community. As CAC feeds the hungry and cares for those in need, the newspaper provides information free to those who need it, no matter who they are.

The symbol of my calling used to be that brown paper bag filled with groceries. Now, my symbol is ink spread across newsprint. It is as mundane as the grocery bag. Yet again I find God in unexpected places as I explore this vocation. Christ comes to me in extraordinary ways, in the most ordinary experiences.

What happened to the question that wove itself through my work those ten years: To be a priest or not?

I've been watching my priest friends carefully. Their lives look pretty much like the rest of us. Some have had great accomplishments, some have suffered tragic losses, and all of them work very hard. Just like anyone, they have a job to do; a calling to answer; a vocation to fulfill. It's still a job I think I could be good at. For now, I'm watching from the pew.

Steven was right after all. If God puts the priesthood in my path, I will know. God will make the next step clear. And as I watch broken, sinful people like me move through the church, I remember it doesn't matter what clothes we wear or where we stand or sit on Sunday mornings—we are all needy for God. If I move toward the priesthood, it will be as a woman still seeking—because we don't answer God's call to solve problems in our lives, we answer because God calls us.

In the years since I've left CAC, people often ask me, "Do you wish you were back?" I answer the question by saying, "'Back' is not the direction I need to be moving."

I do miss the work. I loved my clients and their families. I loved filling empty hands.

There are many stories I didn't write about, stories without endings and stories that are too complicated to explain. Isn't that the way life often is? Without an ending, complicated, and hard to explain.

But when we listen, through silence and through service, God puts the next step in front of us. We don't have to figure out the future. We don't have to fix anyone's life, even our own.

Instead, we will pray, listen, give, and receive with beloved hands. We will look for God in the simple and the surprising and remember that God will come to us, too, in the most remarkable ways. Even in a bag of groceries.

ACKNOWLEDGMENTS

It takes many people to create a book such as this one. There would be no story without the amazing people who came to CAC for help during that decade. You trusted me and loved me. You were Christ to me. Thank you.

I am grateful for my wide circle of family and friends who have been supportive and inspiring. I want to also offer special thanks to the following generous souls.

For quiet, hospitable places to write: Leslie and Dale Richardson, Katie and Don Pearson, and Ginny and Doug Lapins.

For thoughtful early readers of the manuscript: Natalie Cline Bright, Melinda Buza, and Kim Heitzenrater.

For wise advice at critical times: Cameron Tuttle and Lisa Webster, David B. Coe, Laura Brown, Henry Hamman, Bob Short, Jim Turrell, and Sam Williamson.

For unfailing encouragement: Katie Lapins, Spike Willis and Lisa Moore; Lauren Winner, Beth Lincks, Gregory Wolfe and my Glen friends; Wendy and Jack Brown and the "Wendeez," Tami Griffitt, Melissa Webb, Phoebe and Rob Pearigen, Virginia Craighill, Janice and John Thomas, and Geraldine H. Piccard.

For prayerful spiritual direction: Pam Park.

To the loving congregation of Otey Parish and its rector Joe Ballard. Also, those on staff with me during my CAC tenure, including Tom Macfie, Jerrie Lewellen, Betty Carpenter, Beth Charlton, Beverly Powers, Maria Hoecker, Remington Rose-Crossley , and the late Tommy Tate. And to the CAC board and volunteers, including Pixie Dozier, Ann Millar, Henry Chase, Connie Gipson, Cal Winton, John Bratton, Tommy Hewitt, Sarah Cardwell, Sister Elizabeth Mills, and the late Carolyn Hatchett.

For time and support to complete this project: my colleagues at the Sewanee Mountain Messenger, especially Janet Graham, April Minkler, Kiki Beavers, and Sandra Gabrielle.

For editing with grace and precision: Lil Copan and Elisa Stanford.

And most of all, I want to thank my family, who shared these ten years with me: to Addison and Aaron, for their patience and love, and to John, who makes every day a joy for me.

NOTES

Chapter 1: Stepping Out-of-Bounds

1. *The Book of Common Prayer* (New York: Seabury, 1979), 306.

2. Ibid., 305.

Chapter 8: Holy Listening

1. *The Book of Common Prayer* (New York: Seabury, 1979), 392.

2. Contemplative Outreach website: www.contemplativeoutreach. org/category/category/centering-prayer. [Accessed January 18, 2013.]

Chapter 11: Confession and Calling

1. Richard Rohr, *Radical Grace* (Cincinnati: St. Anthony Messenger, 1995), 334.

2. Thomas Keating expressed this description of the distractions we face in his book *Open Mind, Open Heart*, 20th Anniversary edition (New York: Continuum, 2006), 2.

Chapter 12: Miriam's Second Death

1. *The Book of Common Prayer* (New York: Seabury, 1979), 491.